If You Don't Like the Possum, Enjoy the Sweet Potatoes

D1104177

If You Don't Like the Possum, Enjoy the Sweet Potatoes

Some Principles for Travel along the Road of Life

JOHN H. HAYES

CASCADE *Books* · Eugene, Oregon

IF YOU DON'T LIKE THE POSSUM, ENJOY THE SWEET
POTATOES
Some Principles for Travel along the Road of Life

Cascade Books
A Division of Wipf and Stock Publishers
199 W. 8th Ave., Suite 3
Eugene, OR 97401

ISBN 13: 978-1-60608-790-7

Cataloging-in-Publication data:

Hayes, John Haralson, 1934– *2013*
    If you don't like the possum, enjoy the sweet potatoes : some
principles for travel along the road of life / John H. Hayes.

    ISBN 13: 978-1-60608-790-7

    xii + 164 p. ; 23 cm.

    1. Life. 2. Conduct for life. 3. Spirituality. I. Title.

BX9225 H35 2009

Manufactured in the U.S.A.

In memory of

Mattie C.

who kept the faith,
fought the good fight,
endured to the end,
and without whom nothing would have been possible

Contents

Preface

There is little or no order to these midnight meanderings. Like life, they encounter the reader unstructured and in some disarray.

Special thanks are due: my cousins Jerry and John Coggins, who encouraged me throughout the writing; Peter Paulsen (Candler School of Theology); Julie Galambush (College of William and Mary); Wayne Swindall (my pastor); Peter Trudinger (Scots Church, Adelaide, Australia); Paul Swisher (Rock Mills, Alabama), who saved me from many an infelicitous phrase and supplied not a few felicitous ones; and Emory students Kimbrell Teegarden and Bo Adams, who made several valuable suggestions about some of the essays' final form.

J. H. H.

Oftentimes cameo scenes are more enjoyable and artful than the main act.

1 If You Don't Like the Possum, Enjoy the Sweet Potatoes

Throughout the early years of Southern history, and especially during the Great Depression, possum was a major component in the food chain, being a rich source of both protein and calories. Community affairs often featured "possum suppers." On January 19, 1909, for example, the cream of Atlanta society feted president-elect William Howard Taft to a black-tie banquet. The main course was baked possum. In the 1950s, even Southerners, however, generally became too sophisticated to eat possum.

This ubiquitous marsupial was acquired by hunting at night. Dogs treed them. They were located with flashlights. The younger hunters climbed the tree and shook the prey out where another hustled the animal into a burlap sack. Only large specimens were kept. The larger ones were generally caught after midnight, thus leading to the popular expression, "the biggest and best possums roam late in the night."

The captured animals would be caged and fed for a couple of weeks to cleanse out their digestive system and flush out the gamey taste. Cornbread covered with buttermilk was the recommended diet. After being dressed and singed, but not skinned, a possum was baked, surrounded by a horde of peeled sweet potatoes. Exceedingly greasy, the baking possum would fill a house with the tantalizing smell of barbecuing fat. The odor, Southerners say, would make you hit at your granma.

When served on a huge platter, encircled by grease-enriched baked potatoes, the possum looked like a monstrous, naked, brown rat that had expired in the middle of a yam patch. Its appearance, therefore, often curbed the appetites of the hungriest diners, especially children and youngsters. I can remember, as a child, being enthralled at the olfactory but disgusted by the visionary. The sweet potatoes, however, were matters of a different order, and had a taste that was flavorful and mouth-watering, with none of the disturbing appearance of the creature whose fat had made their taste so scintillating. Even those who couldn't gird up the courage to eat the possum could relish the sweet potatoes.

✓ Life often serves us with a dish of possum. The main course in life: job, career, marriage, status, the demands of others, may turn out unappealing and unappetizing. Often we have no other choice than to down the possum. After all, we committed to the matter, as disgusting and boring as it may be, and we have no real exit we can choose or for which we qualify.

Alongside the main dish, however, we're bound to find enjoyable tidbits in life, or at least sufficient stuff that is tasty and nourishing, to make the meal of life not only edible and endurable, but also pleasantly tasteful. Sometimes in life, the accoutrements and the condiments may be preferable to the entrée. The by-products in life may be more enjoyable than the main course. Oftentimes cameo scenes are more enjoyable and artful than the main act. Our avocations may be far more rewarding and satisfying than our vocations; the hobby and the occasional more fun than the required and the habitual.

When it is impossible to like the possum, we should focus on enjoying the sweet potatoes: they can be a meal in themselves.

Don't spend your days setting yourself up as a target on other people's firing ranges.

2 Give People Enough Rope and They Will Hang You

"Give a man enough rope and he will hang himself." So goes the old saying, which surely rests on an optimistic, Pollyanna view of the world. Sometimes it does happen this way and people overcome by greed, envy, hatred, and so on do destroy themselves. Self-execution, however, is relatively rare.

More realistic and expressive of reality is this: if you give people enough rope they will hang you. In Aesop's fable, *The Eagle and the Arrow*, the eagle discovers, too late, that the arrow that brought it down was feathered with its own plume. Aesop's moral: "We often give our enemies the means of our own destruction."

√ We live in an age in which we have been encouraged and admonished to "become vulnerable, not just to our enemies but especially to our friends." We must voluntarily expose ourselves to the possibility of hurt and pain. "Openness" is the highest virtue. Supply everyone with a lengthy roll of rope. In our computer age, with chat rooms and blogging, we can not only reveal our reality but also our virtual reality.

Some people can be pushed to feel shame and guilt if they find themselves harboring some secret. Especially vocal about vulnerability in contemporary society are those who stand to profit from massaging the bruises and clearing up the accidents it leaves in its wake; those for whom divorces and nervous breakdowns represent professional opportunities. There is money to be made "helping" people. One can gain from another's pain.

Humans, even close associates, are nosey, gossipy, and vicious critters. They can feed upon victims and then hold a wake and raise a monument to their memory.

√ Envy, that most widespread and insidious of the cardinal sins, pervades our society, like smog in the city.

Envy reaches its pinnacle in our rejoicing over others' downfalls. Nothing exemplifies this more than the grocery-store media. Every shopper in the checkout line is daily confronted with headlines screaming about others' misdeeds, mistakes, and misfortunes.

✓ In German, the term *Schadenfreude* was coined to refer to the somewhat sadistic pleasure people enjoy at the sight of others' problems. The sight of a social equal, a competitor, and, especially, a superior, in trouble can trigger the joy of an endorphin surge in the brain. In stimulating pleasure, others' failure can be almost as good as, if not better than, one's own success. So, why make oneself overly vulnerable to the benefit of the social vultures?

The human person, like film in a camera, can suffer from over-exposure. Don't spend your days setting yourself up as a target on other people's firing ranges. Don't turn yourself into bait for bigger fish. Voluntary vulnerability ✓ rings hollow anyway. Live a life that is open, honorable, and straightforward, and vulnerability will find you. It is merely the art of being human in the most humane way.

Sit in the parlor with anyone, but limit those who stand around in the kitchen where and when the cooking is being done.

Argue your case with your neighbor directly.

3 Never Attack a Skunk from the Rear

Mephitis mephitis, the skunk, is a member of the weasel family. The dictionary says, it emits "a fetid odor when alarmed or attacked." Fetid is a rarely used word and seems far too mild to refer to the hell of a stink that an angry skunk can apply to anyone or anything in spray range. The smell is worse than that of rotten eggs gone bad.

The evolutionary process endowed this lovely little animal with a rectal auxiliary pouch filled with a liquefied stench as a defense mechanism. When a skunk is cornered, one should never move in to attack the animal from behind since it is equipped to shoot from the rear. Dogs are the most frequent recipients of its douches, often chasing the animal too rapidly to avoid encounter. Any application of skunk fluid leaves an irremovable coating of nasal-disrupting, reeking scent. Applicated clothes are best burned. The smell can be diluted but not extinguished by several thorough bathings with tomato juice.

Much of life is spent skunk dealing. Problems and persons can be the skunks of our existence. Knowing how to approach them and from what direction can make the difference between finesse and fumbling. The objective is to handle matters so as to prevent any odoriferous output or at least to avoid receiving an odoriferous overlay oneself.

Like a farmer circling a skunk in a henhouse, many of us spend time circumambulating. We try to talk out a problem hoping it will die without our having to draw the rapier. We expect the skunk to fall asphyxiated from breathing the heavy fog emitted by our thought and discussion. The playwright, Simon Gray (1936–), has one of his characters say: "In my experience, the worst thing you can do to an important problem is discuss it . . . I really do think this whole business of noncommunication is one of the most poignant fallacies of our zestfully overexplanatory age" (*Otherwise Engaged*, 1975). Many have learned that one of the surest paths to misery is to visit a counselor to discuss a marital problem. Or to appoint a committee to solve a problem.

People with whom we have issues can be cajoled, avoided, placated, and so on. But with these we are still chasing the skunk by going in circles. The wrong attack, the wrong move, and we can end up stinking, a country bumpkin hunting for the tomato juice.

The writer of the biblical book of Proverbs supplies the best approach to troublesome problems and people, to the skunks in our life: "Argue your case with your neighbor directly" (Proverbs 25:9a). You don't stand a chance with a skunk unless you approach it head-on.

Don't spend a life what-
iffing. Learn to bless what is.

4 One-Armed Persons Make Poor Cotton Pickers

During the days of American slavery and throughout the first half of the twentieth century, when labor was cheap and harvesting machines were yet unknown, cotton was picked by hand. The cotton picker, dragging a long sack behind with a strap across the shoulder and over the head, removed the lightly attached fiber from the open boll and sacked it. With dexterity and speed, one could pick up to three hundred pounds a day.

Cotton-picking was a backbreaking, sweaty, low-paying, socially denigrated job. That is why we speak degradingly of someone or something of low quality or painstaking as a cotton-pickin' so and so or such and such.

Incidental pleasures, except for the joy of doing a job well, were few and far between in the cotton fields. I can remember looking forward to getting into high cotton, where the yield was low and the stalks were leafy; to lie down upon my sack and take a nap unseen. Sometimes between rows I came across a stray watermelon vine with a yield of knotty fruit that could be burst with a fist and its meaty innards devoured.

The process of picking often involved using one hand as a temporary storage place before stuffing the cotton into the sack. Occasionally the stalk had to be steadied with one hand while the other picked in spots difficult to access. Such feats made the one-armed person remarkably inept as a fiber plucker.

Life is a cotton-pickin' business. Aptitude, whether for the job at hand or for the career of a lifetime, must be given its role in life. The demands of the task often predetermine the aptitudes required. One short of temper fits poorly a career demanding patience; the overly patient may serve badly in a position demanding quick decisions and immediate action.

Everyone faces some handicaps in life that limit our options—whether physical, financial, or temperamental. A three-hundred pounder can only dream of being the jockey, in the winner's circle, astride a winning racehorse.

✓ Some choices get made for us. Don't waste your time and psychic energy over what might have been, what could have been, what ought to have been. Get on with being. Don't waste your time either fretting about your limitations and lacks or fantasizing about the impossible. Don't spend a life what-iffing. Learn to bless what is.

Self-interest can be of more good to society at large than self-sacrifice.

5 Feed Your Enemy: It's Always Harder to Fight with a Full Stomach

Almost forever parents have warned their children about excessive exertion immediately after eating. "Don't go swimming for thirty minutes after you have eaten!" "Let your lunch settle before you go out to play!" The same perspective should be applied to relations with our enemies: keep them stuffed and they may avoid excessive exertion, like military activity.

Enlightened self-interest, the essence of this attitude, has always been a highly praised ethical posture. Doing good to others for one's own ultimate good is certainly not to be frowned upon.

> If your enemies are hungry,
>> give them bread to eat;
> and if they are thirsty,
>> give them water to drink;
> for you will heap coals of fire on their heads,
>> and the LORD will reward you.
>
> (Proverbs 25:21–22)

This biblical passage doesn't mean one should give food and water in the hopes of singeing your enemy's pate! The expression, "heaping coals upon another's head," probably implies creating in the other a sense of shame or guilt and thus disarmament. The Egyptian *Instruction of Amenemope* (about 1100 BCE) admonished a person in treating an enemy to "fill his belly with bread of yours, so that he shall be satisfied and ashamed." The surest way to a people's mind is through their stomachs. Generosity toward an enemy can confuse your opponent no end.

Nor should acts of enlightened self-interest be dismissed as merely self-serving. Aid to the other in the hope of reciprocation is still aid. "The Lord can give even if the devil delivers."

Self-interest of the even obliquely unenlightened kind can be a benefit and should not be smeared with a broad brush. The Frenchman, François, Duc de la Rochefoucauld (1613–1680), noted that "self-interest speaks all sorts of tongues, and plays all sorts of roles, even that of disinterestedness" (*Reflections; or, Sentences and Maxims*, 1678, maxim 39).

Self-interest supplies us with many goods and services. The Scottish economist, Adam Smith (1723–1790), wrote: "It is not from the benevolence of the butcher, the brewer, or the baker that we expect our dinner, but from their regard to their own interest. We address ourselves, not to their humanity but to their self-love" (*The Wealth of Nations*, 1776). The self-interest of the parents provides opportunities and accouterments for the children.

One could argue that self-interest can be of more good to society at large than self-sacrifice. Self-sacrifice can, after all, be the apogee of self-interest. The early Christian, Bishop Polycarp (69–155 CE) of Smyrna, wanted to be martyred. His only fear was that the teeth of lions might not grind him like grain. He wanted an immediate entry into the heavenly world. Polycarp got his desire. In a way, his martyrdom served the fledging Christian community. His death provided the blood of a martyr, the seed of the church.

The Model-T automobile, on the other hand, a product of the self-interest of Henry Ford (1863–1947), may well have brought more benefit and pleasure to humankind than the death of a hundred martyrs.

No carefully calibrated
amount of lithium can
smooth out the apogees and
nadirs of existence.

6 Life Is Less like a Consommé and More like a Stew

Our lives seldom move on an even keel nor sail on a wave-free sea. No carefully calibrated amount of lithium can smooth out the apogees and nadirs of existence. Life is a stew not a consommé.

Consommé is made so as to be consistent throughout. The first spoonful and the last spoonful, and all the spoonfuls in between, are made to look and taste the same. A stew is the opposite, a mixture of materials, tastes, and textures. Life is much more stew-like than consommé-like: a conglomeration of tasty morsels, solids, liquids, lumps, clumps, and sometimes a tough sinew or gristle. It is a mixture of opposites and everything in between; both yin and yang. Life is ups and downs, light and darkness, joy and sorrow, exaltation and depression, success and failure, work and play. We need the yin to yang and the yang to yin.

Nowhere is the stew-like quality of life better expressed than in the traditional marriage ceremony. The participants pledge themselves to one another for better or worse, for richer or poorer, in sickness and in health—that is, in all the multifarious forms through which existence presents itself.

By the time we reach middle age the stew of life has provided us with a bag, a treasure store, of memories. Memories that we recall with both gladness and sadness.

There is much to show gladness over: the care and provision our parents provided, even when not very good, were probably the best they could do; making it through that first day of school in a new world so alien and threatening; a new pair of shoes that allowed us to strut like a peacock; standing triumphantly on first base, astride the bag as if we were some warrior returned victoriously from battle even though our grounder had only dribbled its way past the outstretched hands of some other uncoordinated youngster; receiving diplomas certifying our learning; the mittened fingers of another that caressed the snowflakes from our eyelashes; the first time ever we saw that face; the first squeeze from a hand we felt destined to clasp and to hold forever; the opening in our heart through which only one would fit; the time when two hearts melted, flowed together, and congealed into a new entity whose pulsating throbs could sustain the life and passion of two; those first days of marriage when our lust met its satiety; the first time we held a diapered hunk of humanity bearing our genes; cats that cuddle and sleep on our laps; dogs anxious to please and faithfully forgiving and forgetting; the medications that eased our pain and calmed our troubled brain; the times we confronted temptation face to face, stared it straight in the eye and turned and walked away; seeing loved ones move through the shadow of death and exit into the sunshine of life; recollections of those departed that tiptoe through the shadows of our memory; those occasions when generosity could be extended anonymously; those times when we reached out and another reached in.

Amid the mix, there is much to show sadness over: dedication we did not devote; effort we did not exert; the dreams we refused to trust; caution that kept us chained to the ordinary; thoughts we suppressed and left unspoken and so unheard; roads we did not travel; paths we did not tread; passages we did not open through the thickets of life; the times we confronted temptation face to face, and threw aside our inhibitions and ran to embrace it; weak wills incapable of motivating us into action; love we did not clearly articulate nor adequately embody; hugs we did not grant; tears we did not shed; pain and misery we did not share; the sorrow too deep for tears and the hurt too deep for pain; the times we convinced ourselves that happiness was an adequate substitute for contentment; the times we confused dependence with friendship; the despair through which we could not work and which still accompanies us like an unwanted hitchhiker; hopes and dreams lying shriveled, exhausted from over assertion and under achievement; forgiveness we did not request; forgiveness we did not grant; praise we did not offer; thanks we did not express; times when the other reached out and we never reached in; color lines we did not cross; barriers we did not tear down; movements we did not join; the times when we were not among those who stood up to be counted; friendships we neither cultivated nor watered and which withered, drooped, and died in our very presence; indignation we did not vent; those gone we did not bid adieu.

✓ Life's stew undeniably includes a healthy share of lumps and sinews to be chewed and swallowed. But even the toughest bits, over time, are simmered in the broth of our interaction, made tender by the care and forgiveness of others and of ourselves.

It's a lumpy sort of life, a sweet-and-sour mix of gifts and losses, rich enough to challenge and sustain us until the end.

A major problem with true believers is that they will roll their truth into a stick, and use it to beat the hell out of you.

7 Certitude Is the Breeding Ground of Intolerance and Violence

Throughout history, society has often respected, even venerated, persons who are "true believers," people who know what they believe, who do not tolerate doubt in themselves, and who are committed to a program of enlightening and indoctrinating everybody else. Such believers have discovered or been discovered by "the truth." Their goal in life is to create a world in which everyone enjoys the benefits of their correct belief and its corollary of ideal behavior. Such a positive outlook supplies not only singleness of vision but also long nights of contented sleep, nestled deep and comfortable in the down of blessed assurance. Although such confidence may be fed by hidden and unconscious springs of uncertainty, such doubts are nothing compared with the rushing torrents of knowing what is both true and right.

True belief may be built around politics, economics, culture, or religion. Often it is a mixture of more than one. The true believer knows what political system is best for the entire world and best for the individuals of that world. The true American believer knows that if everyone in the world could have their own constitution, get the right to vote, and express their God-given freedoms then utopia would be just around the corner.

For others, the issues are more economical. Society should operate so as either to encourage individual expression and accomplishment to the fullest, with everyone standing on their own two feet, living and dying by their own achievement; or, on the other hand, so as to extinguish all individual activity and achievement that clash with the common good and that allow the elevation of one person above another.

Cultural true believers know how people should behave, what clothes they should wear, how their hair should be combed, how they should express themselves, and on and on.

The world's most ardent are of course the religious true believers, confident in their own certitude and certain that others are outside the pale. The medieval church knew it possessed the truth, the whole truth, and nothing but the truth and that outside its embrace the world was populated with heathens, all hell-bound.

A major problem with true believers is that they will roll their truth into a stick, and use it to beat the hell out of you. True believers affirm their validity by denying that of others. An early Christian Crusader wrote home, bragging that he had ridden his horse in the courtyards of Solomon's temple knee-deep in the blood of Muslim infidels. Within the medieval and early modern church, possessors of radical or different ideas were frequently tied to the stake, to die inhaling the smoke of their own barbecuing flesh. But, of course, all this was done to protect the truth and to save the soul of the sautéed.

Carrying the banner of truth, true believers have always campaigned to overlay the world with their perspectives and to create everyone else in their own image. They do not appreciate the fact that life is a journey not a campaign. As we make the journey, we may occasionally catch glimpses of the truth but we frequently don't realize what we have seen until the landscape has already changed.

St. Paul wrote to the Corinthians: "we see through a glass darkly" (or "now we see in a mirror, dimly"; 1 Corinthians 13:4). True believers, in contrast, see through a constantly clean window, live in the light of a blazing sun, and set out with truth in hand and a goal in view. They transform everything into a battle, a campaign for their right belief. But surely we live in a world where doubt should not be viewed as an indication of weakness but as a sign of integrity.

Shouldn't we hold our truth more gently, squeeze it with a loose grip, and hope that we are not in the way when the crusade of true believers, the storm troopers of righteousness and orthodoxy, arrives where we live?

There is no learner's permit for parenthood.

8 Try to Live so Your Children Won't Want to Piss on Your Tombstone

Interpersonal relationships are always complex, if not complicated. Few human relations are more complex and intertwined than those of the family. Sociologists inform us that the vast majority of families may be classified as dysfunctional. This means that they do not operate to maximize human potential and to provide caring and exemplary nurture. Such an assessment is nothing new. The authors of the Bible depicted even the first human family as colossally dysfunctional. Adam and Eve would not live under obligation; they would not accept responsibility for their own actions; they blamed each other for their problems; they listened to and took directions from some creepy snake; and their oldest child killed the second-born (after falling out over religion!).

By its very nature, parenthood suffers since parents have to get training while already on the job. There is no learner's permit for parenthood. You never have time to learn. You are thrown into a game already underway. No child comes into the world with a tag sewn to its fanny, like a mattress, telling you how to rear it and not to remove the tag under penalty of law. In spite of a desire to do the best job possible, what good parenting is and how to do it are unknowns. Parents often feel themselves as actors in a series of one-day dramas directed by their offspring.

A major problem with childrearing is that it takes place under natural and normal conditions, that is, when people tend to act and behave as the people they really are. Facades don't work at home. The kids have even seen us in the bathroom, sitting astride the commode. As a result, children witness their parents "homely" looking. Often they experience them as concerned, caring, and compassionate. But they also see them scheming, fudging on matters, lying, charading, and who knows what else. They witness

24

their parents' anger, jealousy, passions, and pettiness—and often are the object of these. Many parents are like the cat that stays outdoors for hours only to rush straight to the litter box when readmitted: they save their dirtiest stuff for home.

All of us injure and scar our children in one way or another, sometimes seriously. An alcoholic parent, without the will or the capability to confront reality, who tries to drown their problems or dull the pain with drink, may program their children to flee from reality. Since children always watch and listen to their parents, habits, especially the bad ones, are picked up like a sponge soaking up water.

Sometimes children have to learn and do on their own, because of parental unwillingness or incapacity. My son always wanted to build things. Since I could hardly tell a screwdriver from a wrench, I never sought to nor could I have taught him carpentry. In spite of my ineptitude, he taught himself after leaving home and is today a great woodworker.

Parenting should be understood as employment, something your children have hired you to do. Such employment ought to be treated with respect, honesty, and responsibility. "Good" parents live up to their employment responsibilities; but unlike other employers, children are caring and forgiving, if given the chance. Parents should embody and manifest those qualities and virtues they desire in their children. The goal of parenthood is to launch competent and conscientious children into the mainstream of life.

Many children don't witness parents as caring, honest, demanding, and forgiving. Instead they see and experience something else, ranging from neglect to abuse. Out of such seeing and experiencing, respect disappears. Parents should be as self-conscious about parenting as they are about their work and vocation. Many children, if they expressed their true, and often legitimate sentiments, would not visit deceased parents in the cemetery and, if they did, instead of an arrangement of colorful plastic flowers, they would leave behind expressions of pain and disappointment and often a few manifestations of anger. Many a tear shed at a funeral has flowed down the cheeks of a face harboring an unexpressed, smirky smile.

One should so live that those plastic representations of love that decorate our cemeteries will not be the result of shame and guilt, but can be an embodiment of respect.

The entire apparatus of human civility may be viewed as the imposition of regulations on methane expulsion.

9 Nobody Is Ever Greatly Bothered by Their Own Personally-Produced Methane

Human beings, like all other animals, are born with a drive to survive, a will to live. In the evolutionary nature of things, there is no other way to make it in this world. We have to be self-centered, to demand that our needs be met. Selfishness is as normal as breathing. The cry of the infant is the voice of survival. That demand for a two o'clock feeding is a declaration: "I must thrive even if no one else should survive."

The innocence of babies results not from purity of heart but rather from weakness. They do not possess the strength to act as they might wish. As Saint Augustine (354–430) wrote: "The weakness of little children's limbs is innocent, not their souls" (*Confessions*).

The urge to survive and the self-centeredness of existence soon encounter the strictures and structures that socialize the person into, hopefully, a being that can co-exist with others and fit into and contribute to the larger society. Humanity has laid upon us all at least a modicum of requirements and demands.

In our drive to survive, we develop behavior and habits, some of which that larger socializing entity to which we belong will not approve, nor would it care to endure. Take, for instance, flatulence. Each of us are great methane producing machines. The private expulsion of our own methane gas does not cause distress or displeasure to us personally. Other people's methane, however, is highly unpleasant, since we have not become acclimated to either the aroma or its distinctive qualities. We can endure our own but are bothered by others'. Flatulence in public is no way to win friends, although it can certainly influence people. One doesn't have to be Marshall McLuhan (1911–1980) to realize that with flatulence, "the medium is the message."

The entire apparatus of human civility may be viewed as the imposition of regulations on methane expulsion. How we handle our methane can be seen as a cipher for how we relate to others. Socially acceptable and socially sanctioned behavior places demands, boundaries, and strictures on each of us. One's methane (like other aspects of our lives), although not found to be personally obnoxious, should not be exuded so as to disrupt and disgust social relations.

What applies to methane also applies to a multitude of other matters.

The products of our industry, our personal achievements, and our personal qualities are fair game for the male dogs who run among us.

10 If You Own a Male Dog, Eat the Fruit from High off the Tree

Anyone who has ever planted and nurtured a fruit tree knows how anxiously you await the joy of eating its first produce. The first to mature and ripen may not be the best the tree can produce, but poor quality and taste are overshadowed by the pleasure of enjoying the first fruits of one's labor.

I watched as a first fig struggled toward maturity. When the day arrived and the fig finally looked edible, I set out to garner the initial harvest. Walking toward the tree, I was bypassed by my old male hound. He ran to the tree, lifted his back right leg, and bathed the fig in a shower of urine. Had I made my harvest five minutes later, I might never have known all the truth, although I might have wondered about that fig's taste. The object lesson was clear: if you own a male dog, eat fruit that has grown above the spray line, or wash thoroughly before consuming.

One has to watch out for the male dogs, the urinators in life. They often spray dissonance and distortion on anything and everything. The products of our industry, our personal achievements, and our personal qualities are fair game for the male dogs who run among us. It is so easy for all of us to turn others and their achievements into figs or fire hydrants.

Reaching for gratification
in the present . . . can leave
us warming ourselves
by the fires of burning
bridges, by the embers of
our squandered potentials,
and by the ashes of our
unrealized achievements.

11 Don't Burn Your Bridges Before You Cross Them

A bridge has almost forever been a metaphor for transition. Bill Clinton campaigned for president talking about building a bridge to the twenty-first century.

An old folk adage admonishes us not to "burn our bridges behind us." This warning reminds us that the most strategic maneuver, given the proper circumstances, may be retreat. Under such conditions we need to retrace our moves so as to begin again. In other contexts, this saying warns us not to cut off our connection with the past—our culture, our place of origin, our family, our associates, that is, what gave us life and sustained and shaped our existence.

We would all like to have or to be "a bridge over troubled water" (Paul Simon, 1942–). (All of us also wish we had come up with that phrase!)

Another saying that employs bridge imagery is the adage "Don't cross the bridge before you come to it." Such advice—like "Don't count your chickens before they hatch" or "Don't count your eggs before they are laid"—warns us not to assume that the outcome will always equal our expectations. Awaited promises are not established premises. And we all know that we should not waste effort and resources "building bridges to nowhere."

Many of us are guilty of burning our bridges before we cross them. Our actions in the present can sabotage our options for the future.

There are three basic requirements for achievement ✓ in life. (1) One needs to inherit a reasonably good set of genes from one's parents. (2) One needs to be willing to do a bit more than the task at hand requires. Nothing special can or should be gained from merely meeting normal requirements and expectations. (3) One must be willing to postpone self-gratification, forever if necessary.

Failure to adhere to the third of these so often endangers our future and burns our bridges before we cross them. The Bible contains a story about the twins Esau and Jacob (Genesis 25:19–34) in which the oldest, Esau, sells his birthright for a bowl of stew. To fill his stomach and quench his hunger immediately overrode his potential future status.

Reaching for gratification in the present, when we fall prey to our own appetites, whether with "irrational exuberance" (Alan Greenspan, 1926–) or with weak wills merely seeking indulgence or with shortsighted vision, can leave us warming ourselves by the fires of burning bridges, by the embers of our squandered potentials, and by the ashes of our unrealized achievements.

Maybe the change in perspective will improve the view and the disposition of the spirit.

12 Commuting is Never Back and Forth but Always Forth and Back

Ask weary commuters and they will all tell you that they go "back and forth" to work. Of course, none of them do. You cannot come back from where you have not gone. One must first "go forth" and then return by "coming back."

The expression "back and forth" probably originated from the action of using a rocking chair. Sitting down, one starts the process of rocking by pushing backward after which the chair, moved by the weight of its occupant and the curvature of its runners, not only returns to its upright position but also tips forward, giving us that rocking pleasure. A swing, of course, works in the same manner. Traveling to and from work never functions this way.

So, quit commuting back and forth and get to commuting forth and back. Maybe the change in perspective will improve the view and the disposition of the spirit. Why start out in reverse and predetermine the movement in the negative? "To go forth" has an optimistic ring, an openness about it, especially when it is the initial move.

Ontogeny recapitulates phylogeny.

13 That Nightmare May Be Uncle Og and Aunt Ig Fleeing from a Saber-toothed Tiger

For thousands of years before humans became the predators, they were the prey. Our earliest ancestors were berry and nut pickers and scavengers, perhaps only occasionally slaughtering something on their own. Humans were merely atoms in the larger molecule of life. They were not so much the hunters as the hunted, not killing but trying not to be killed. Fear, fright, and flight must have been not only their constant companions, but also ingrained into their very genes, to be transmitted to all subsequent descendants.

As the latest link in the evolutionary chain extending backwards to that time when "men were first produced in fishes, and when they were grown and able to help themselves, were thrown up, and so lived upon the land" (Anaximander, about 611–547 BCE), each of us carries in our physical, mental, and emotional makeup the prints and patterns of all our predecessors. Biologists have an expression, "ontogeny recapitulates phylogeny," which is a claim that each individual specimen in a species reproduces the entire evolutionary process of the species as a whole. All the multiple stages of development are replicated in the single individual who is an embodiment of the whole.

When we awake at night horrified by some hideous nightmare, filled with inexplicable angst, we may simply be re-living our ancestors' flight from danger. Those cold sweats that once decorated the hairy physique of some primordial, stooped anthropoid fleeing for safety, running bow-legged with knuckles bouncing on the ground, may re-form upon our brows. In our irrational, desperate fear we may again be joining that flight to avoid becoming the prey. We should find consolation in knowing that we are simply sharing with Uncle Og and Aunt Ig, our primordial ancestors, a will to live, to survive, to reach that tree before the tiger's teeth tear through our flesh and we become a meal. We should find soothing comfort in the realization that since we are here, Uncle Og and Aunt Ig must have made it. If they did, so can we.

The cannibal cook has finished; the cooked cannibal is done.

14 Meat Gets Done, People Get Finished

"Are you done?" "I'm almost done." Such expressions are heard every day. When we complete a job, we say we are done; what we really mean is we have finished. When a cannibal cooks a compatriot, roasting or boiling the person to taste, then after checking the flesh's temperature, the cannibal can say, "He is done." The cannibal's cooking chore is "finished"; his compatriot, the evening meal, is "done." The cannibal cook has finished; the cooked cannibal is done.

The words we choose, the terminology we employ, how we put all these together, all speak volumes about not only our own self-understanding but also what we think about and how we evaluate those to whom we speak. Always try to use grammar correctly even when you are merely explaining to another how to cook a cousin.

We must all walk a
lonesome road, alone.

15 Every Person Is an Island

The English theologian and poet John Donne (1573–1631) wrote in his *Devotion upon Emergent Occasions* (1624), that ✓ "no man is an island." Like all great, memorable sayings, this one embodies an easily recognizable insight: we all live interrelated lives, interconnected with, and interdependent on, others. None of us could live or become a person without community. It may not take a village to form and educate a child but each needs the other.

Such universalizing sayings, as this one of Donne, however, distort reality and submerge insights. They should not be allowed to silence the opposite of their totalizing insight. We all know, of course, that such nuggets of wisdom are time, circumstance, and place conditioned. Every culture has proverbs with totally contrary meanings: ✓ "The one who hesitates is lost," but be sure to "look before you leap."

Each of us *is* an island—alone, isolated, awash in the waters of our own private sea. Regardless of those interpersonal umbilicals through which we find support and nourishment, and sometimes bad sustenance, we ultimately decide, stand, and act alone. The ports we enter are the ports we chose to enter.

> It matters not how strait the gate,
> > How charged with punishments the scroll,
> I am the master of my fate:
> > I am the captain of my soul.

> —William Ernest Henley (1849–1905, English poet and critic)

Even amid the pressure of our peers, even when ensconced in the standards and mores of our social context, even when impelled by raging hormones and beckoned by scintillating expectations, even when encouraged by our associates or our financial advisers, our thoughts and actions are ultimately ours alone. Under orders, even when broken by discipline, a soldier's decision is a soldier's decision. At the deepest level of existence, we must all walk a lonesome road, alone. In the final hour, we may die holding each other's hands, but we die singularly, alone.

The flotsam and jetsam that wash up upon the shores of our lives are seldom the sole consequence of the archipelago in which we live; the garbage and debris that litter the beaches of our personal lives are generally of our own creation.

No one is an island, yet everyone is an island.

Few people seem to know
more about the conditions
to prevail in and the
geography and demography
of the world beyond
than uneducated and
unsophisticated clerics and
gospel singers ill at ease in
the world of the present . . .

16 Visions of the Hereafter Should Not Distort the View of the Here-and-Now

Throughout the western Christian tradition, people have talked about "dying and going to heaven." Such an expression, and probably its sentiments, is never found in the Bible, the foundation document of the Christian religion. Whether human views about life after death have been a blessing or a bane is a debatable but ultimately insoluble issue. But clearly too strong a focus on the hereafter can be a plague on life in the here-and-now.

Karl Marx (1818–1883) castigated religion with its proclamation of the blessings of the beyond often promised amid the squalor of the present. He wrote: "Religion is the sigh of the oppressed creature, the feelings of a heartless world, just as it is the spirit of unspiritual conditions. It is the opium of the people" (*Introduction to a Critique of Hegelian Philosophy*, 1844). Whether belief in a hereafter is primarily a crutch that makes movement through this world possible, a cushion that softens the blows of existence, or a means of convincing the oppressed to endure the agony of the here by feeding on the promise of the there, is of course impossible to know.

As a human motivator, belief in rewards and punishments in a world to come has been and can be a powerful force. It can undergird the willingness of a terrorist to splatter not only his or her own flesh and blood but also that of others in all directions and allow such a one to die awaiting the virginal embrace of heavenly nymphs. It can lead one to self-denial, to self-depression, to a surrender of self-enhancement in this world in the expectation of a complete reversal in that other world. Many seek to surrender all forms of greed and desire in this life, gambling that in the future their status will be reversed and they will be the beneficiaries of an eschatological death policy, leaving behind the misery of their indentured lives.

Normal greed in this world can be postponed in the hope ✓ of a fully realized supernatural greed in the world to come with its rewards, crowns, and "a mansion just over the hilltop."

Few people seem to know more about the conditions to prevail in and the geography and demography of the world beyond than uneducated and unsophisticated clerics and gospel singers ill at ease in the world of the present who draw their theologies from lyrics written in New Orleans or Nashville. This should give us pause for thought.

Conditions in and even the potential of life beyond this life remain mysterious unknowns. The world we now ✓ inhabit, however, is immediately at hand. Our life here and now, the potentials it provides, and the problems that need addressing, should never be glazed over in the hope of avoiding present reality or in the expectation of sliding gently into that world to come.

We must live, labor, laugh, and love in the present tense, and circumscribe our hopes in some future pluperfect tense.

In confession we supply the colors to repaint our self-portrait.

17 Sometimes the Most Nourishing Diet for the Soul Is to Eat Crow

Traditional lore has it that the reference to "eating crow" originated in the War of 1812. A British and an American soldier, through a series of coincidental events, each forced the other to eat a crow at a time when other game was not available. In the South, in rural, poverty-stricken areas, young crows shot and killed while still nestlings have occasionally provided supplemental fare for bare tables. To refer to someone as a crow-eater placed him or her on the lower rungs of the economic ladder.

"To eat crow" now denotes having to do something disagreeable, being forced to face aspects of one's self and one's actions that don't reflect well on the person. Often it has to do with facing reality when our performance does not measure up to our braggadocio. We have to eat our words.

The most serious and significant form of crow consumption involves us in genuine confession of our wrongdoings. Confession—"good for the soul and bad for the reputation"—can be one of the most difficult and disagreeable acts we ever undertake, but it is sometimes the most necessary.

Confession, with its attendant sidekick, repentance, has not always been a recommended course. In fact, it has often been disdained. The English poet John Dryden (1631–1700) wrote: "Repentance is the virtue of weak minds," and "Repentance is but want of power to sin." Others have offered advice on the matter, which in practice may not aid the troubled soul: "Repent one day before your death" (Rabbi Eliezer, Mishnah, *Aboth* 2:10); "To do it no more is the truest repentance" (Martin Luther, 1483–1546).

Alcoholics Anonymous has made self-assessment, confession, and restitution central to its program. This organization recognizes what the Italian dramatist Vittorio

Alfieri (1749–1803) expressed: "To err is human; but contrition felt for the crime distinguishes the virtuous from the wicked." Even that old rascal Voltaire (1694–1778) could declare (although he doesn't seem to have followed his own advice), "We all go astray, but the least imprudent is he who the earliest comes to repent." Publilius Syrus (first century BCE) declared that "confession of our faults is the next thing to innocence."

✓ True confession is motivated by an inner crisis of the soul, by genuine remorse and regret, by the moment when it becomes unbearable any longer to suffocate the drive to purge the conscience so that one can hopefully begin anew. In confession we supply the colors to repaint our self-portrait. Confession helps to right the self with itself.

Confession, of course, must be distinguished from acknowledgment or admission that comes when one has no other choice. The child caught in the cookie jar; the criminal convicted in court; the politician who says, "I am responsible," but never specifies nor acts; the TV evangelist caught in the whorehouse; they make admission and acknowledgment but not confession. Those caught cannot confess but only admit. They may name the crow, but they do not eat it!

Every person's suffering
and pain are unique,
stamped with the image of
individuality.

18 Real Empathy Occurs When Other People's Tears Flow Down Our Cheeks

Pity, sympathy, and empathy are all closely related, yet uniquely distinct. Pity is to feel personal horror and sadness over another's plight and suffering. It is a subjective feeling, felt inwardly. Pity says, "The condition of that person/ situation is terrible." Sympathy involves feeling some identity with another. It is a willingness to share the feelings of another, to harmonize with another's plight. Sympathy says, "I would hate to be in that condition." Empathy involves an identification with, a vicarious sharing of the other's feelings, thoughts, and attitudes. Empathy says, "I can feel something of that person's pain and misery." Pity produces a feeling *about* the other, sympathy a feeling *for* the other, and empathy a feeling *with* the other.

All three of these are to be esteemed. They can create in us not only a sense of compassion and care but also stimulate us into action, into deeds that may alleviate a misfortune or its cause.

All my childhood and teenage years were spent in a segregated South. As the son of a sharecropper, options were few and far between, luxuries only a dream. Playmates for myself and my younger brother were almost all African-American children in the neighborhood (of course, in those days, linguistically correct language was never heard). We played baseball till darkness fell, whenever possible. We would make a ball with some old, worn-out socks wrapped around a small rock, all encased in black electric tape (always a scarcity!). The handle of a worn-out broom or a roughly shaped tree limb served as a bat. At play and on the field we were merely human boys sharing and enjoying life without boundaries.

Our worlds were nonetheless different even though we shared common bonds of care and competition. They always came to the back door to announce their presence for a game and ate their meals outside or on the porch. We wore second-hand clothes; they wore third-hand.

The social system functioned to open a door out for me. For them, the door was always slammed shut and bolted. The cards were dealt by society to give me a playing hand but to make sure they lost. When I think of what life offered me and what life offered them, I cannot help but grieve. Most were better ballplayers than I. Our IQs were not radically different. The equality we knew in that cow-pasture baseball game ended there. Any effort they might have exerted to achieve the vision of a better future was hampered by the shackles from the past and the obstacles of the present. For them any vision of the future was blurry. The guilt of success still haunts me; sadness over what life offered them and the system that smothered any flicker of their hope makes me cry.

We often hear people say that we should "walk a mile in the other's shoes" in order to appreciate fully the other's predicament. That is, we must experience what they experience, but that, of course, is impossible. Such a mile would be walked with feet that are strangers to the shoes. To say to another, "I know *exactly* how you feel," is to hand them a bucket of hogwash or hot spit; it is banging on an empty cymbal. Even the most sincere empathy cannot produce identity; it cannot incarnate us in the flesh and spirit of another. A feeling *with* is still not a feeling *of*. Every person's suffering and pain are unique, stamped with the image of individuality. Perhaps the best we can do is to reach the point where we can let others' tears moisten our cheeks. The contours of the world can be radically changed when viewed through the prisms of our or others' tears. Tears have a way of melting the ice and corroding the metal in which we encase our hearts.

If we are true to others, then it must follow, as the night the day, we can never be false to ourselves.

All of us will someday develop an allergy to the smoke of birthday candles.

19 The Older We Get, the Weirder Our Toenails Grow

Much has been written about old age, the elderly, and aging, often by those who view it from a distance. It has, at times, been idealized by philosophers and thinkers who were better poets than observers of the human condition. We are taught how to avoid it, how to prepare for it, how to enjoy it, how much freedom it gives us, how much wiser it makes us, how it transports us beyond the passions of our youth and the mistakes of our middle age. We hear extolled the value of old wine, old wood, old books, and old friends.

Realists have always known that the main problem with the elderly is that they are old and diminished and that old age is a condition from which no one recovers. Robert Browning (1812–1889) must have been whistling in the dark when he wrote, "Grow old along with me! The best is yet to be . . ."; as was Seneca (c. 4 BCE—65 CE), who suggested, "Life is most delightful when it is on the downward slope"; or Oliver Wendell Holmes (1800–1894), speaking on the seventieth birthday of Julia Ward Howe (27 May 1889), who declared: "To be seventy years young is something far more cheerful and hopeful than to be forty years old." The realist, Greek biographer, Bion (c. 325–255 BCE), declared, according to Diogenes Laertius (*Lives of Eminent Philosophers* IV.47), that "old age is the harbor of all ills" may have been nearer to marking the course of our destiny. All of us will someday develop an allergy to the smoke of birthday candles.

We probably all shall experience old age differently. For some, autumn will be a better season than springtime. For some the graying mare will be the better horse. For others, the fruit, already overly ripe, will slowly or even quickly rot away. Some of us will be destined to become drooling, driveling, dilapidated, skin-encased sacks of depleted DNA. We will all experience that anatomical status where our working parts either rust out, break apart, fall off, or clog up. All our old memories will become faded, isolated snapshots without a narrative context. The guidelines to the anchors of our existence will fray and unravel. Our "senior moments" will increase in frequency, intensity, and longevity. Sooner or later, we shall all become preoccupied with bladder management, 24–7–365. For many, the December of life will be without the joys of either Hanukkah or Christmas.

For all of us, at least one thing is inevitable regardless of how old age has embraced us: the older we get the more peculiarly our toenails will grow. Not by accident, boards of wood attached by driving nails at an oblique angle are called "toe-nailed." Nails that once adorned our feet and aided us in walking become in old age problems with which pedicurists and podiatrists struggle. Instead of growing straight ahead, they burrow to the side seeking to hide beneath quick flesh. Ridges appear as if some subterranean mountain chain was encased underneath struggling to free itself. Ends curl and between clippings never grow the same. Trying to trim them, reaching over an expanded gut, fishing to catch a foot somewhere down there, can leave you asphyxiated, gasping for oxygen.

The weirdness of our toenail growth is one of those signs of inevitability; a reminder that it is often harder to walk downhill than up. If all those philosophizing about old age had spent more time contemplating their toenails, they might have written more useful advice.

Cursing the dark gives us,
for a time, the ego strength
we need to mold the tallow,
trim the wick, and locate a
match.

20   First Curse the Dark, Then Light a Candle

When calamity falls and darkness envelops the soul, there is little consolation in being told to look on the bright side, to hope for the best, to light a candle, to energize the power of positive thinking. These may ultimately be worth doing but not when initially groping to find one's bearing and to assess one's condition.

Sudden disruptions and disorientations—abandonment, accidents, depression, and disease—often strike without warning and with no rational discernable cause. Calamity and catastrophe can ambush us amid the common and the normal. When these strike and we find ourselves without a toehold, much less a solid foundation on which to stand, despair and hopelessness immediately become our companions.

The weakness, desperation, aloneness, and anger that despair engenders can momentarily debilitate us. It is no use pretending otherwise. In such a time, lashing out verbally at that formless enemy which has brought us into the buffetings of fate can be as natural as breathing—and as healthy.

The authors who wrote the biblical psalms knew that on occasion we must see even God as the enemy and speak to the Creator accordingly. The psalmists allowed worshipers to accuse God, to plead with God to leave them alone, to get off their case, and just to let them live outside the divine presence for a time (see Psalm 39).

In speaking of the Holocaust, Elie Wiesel (1928–) wrote: "I was the accuser, God the accused. My eyes were open and I was alone—terribly alone in a world without God and without man" (*Night*, 1958).

I was commuting to the university, as I so often did, two hours before dawn and driving, as people frequently do, in a semi-comatose state. A black cat suddenly darted from the roadside into the highway. My left front tire struck the animal solidly. At the next driveway, I turned the car around to return to the scene, hoping, if nothing else, to remove the body so traffic would not pound its lifeless body into a thin, hairy pelt. The cat was nowhere to be seen, only a spot of blood marking the place of encounter. For a time, I parked alongside the highway.

Images flooded my mind: an injured cat suffering and dying alone in the woods; some young child for whom that cat might have been a bosom buddy; some elderly person for whom that cat might have been the sole source of companionship; Midnight, one of my own cats, that hours earlier had slept the night cuddled safely between my feet. What if it was a mother, out scavenging for food to feed itself and sustain some small litter of kittens, secreted away in a hidden crevice somewhere?

There was no candle to light so I cursed the dark: the darkness that had rendered the black cat invisible; the invention of the automobile that had led to such invasion of the creaturely world; the fact that I had momentarily, unknowingly, and unwillingly become an instrument of evil, destruction, and death. Through my tears I could see no light, but at least I had not undergone the experience and yet remained comatose. The remainder of the road to school seemed to stretch out with no end.

One must, therefore, disagree with the motto of the Christopher Society, "it is better to light one candle than curse the darkness." It is often better first to curse the dark, then to light a candle. Cursing the dark gives us, for a time, the ego strength we need to mold the tallow, trim the wick, and locate a match.

Life often gives by the foot,
and takes by the yard.

21 Learn to Buy High and Sell Low

The old financial adage reminds us to "buy low and sell high." This way you are assured not only of recovering your investment but also of making a profit. Success is the goal. And it is true that as long as you are buying low and selling high, things look pretty good. Nobody ever commits suicide because they made a killing on the stock market. Sunny days are seldom depressing.

What we need to worry about, think about, and plan about is the reverse: buying high and having to sell low; moving out not moving up; enduring downward mobility, failure, and underemployment. For most in life, the problem is not speeding but lack of traction. We buy at the wedding, and we sell at the funeral. For many, life is not so much like "a tale told by an idiot, full of sound and fury" (Shakespeare, *Macbeth*) but a tale untold, full of anonymity and oblivion. Life often gives by the foot, and takes by the yard. For some people life resembles a sleepover at The Bates Motel.

Books of inspirational quotes are stuffed with hopeful sayings and cheery advice, most of it merely dressed-up denials that failures are failures. Yet, as Elizabeth Oakes Smith (1806–1893), in her poem *The Unattained* (1843) wrote:

> Yes, this is life; and everywhere we meet,
> Not victor crowns, but wailings of defeat.

Life is not the *opera exceptionelle* destined to end with a hallelujah chorus and a cast of characters who live happily ever after. Instead, all our hopes and dreams seem to pass through Dealey Plaza.

Any dumb, old jackass can enjoy the warmth and comfort of the barn; it is those rainy nights in the open, chilling wind that are the problem. Robert Frost (1874–1963), in *The Death of a Hired Man*, wrote about the time when there was "nothing to look backward to with pride, and nothing to look forward to with hope." There are times when life gives you nothing to say grace over. That is when we need help, and pious platitudes do not supply sustenance to a famished soul. Give us fewer books with titles like *The Power of Positive Thinking* and more books with titles like *Failing but Still Surviving*, or *Failure: How to Make the Most of It*, or *Hanging on When You Had Rather Be Hanging Out*.

Biblical law allowed the community to stone to death an incorrigible son.

22 Bless the Day You Realized that Your Children, after All, Had Finally Become Adults

The parent-child relationship has been much praised and as often maligned. In antiquity, children were the promise of social security in old age. They were laborers in the field and thus a substitute for hired workers. They offered protection at home and gave social status to the parents.

> Sons (children) are indeed a heritage from the LORD,
>   the fruit of the womb, a reward.
> Like arrows in the hand of a warrior
>   are the sons (children) of one's youth.
> Happy is the man who has
>   his quiver full of them.
> He shall not be put to shame
>   when he speaks with his enemies in the gate.
> (Psalm 127:3–5)

The ancients also knew, as do we, that parent-child relationships could sour. Mesopotamian law allowed a parent to sell a disobedient son into slavery. Biblical law allowed the community to stone to death an incorrigible son (Deuteronomy 21:18–21).

The parent-child relationship has often been the topic of humor, attempting to dull the sharp edge of reality. "Insanity is inherited, you get it from your children." "Parents are the bones on which children sharpen their teeth" (Peter Ustinov, 1921–2004; *Dear Me*, 1977).

One of the most rewarding days in a parent's life comes when you can relate to your child as an adult, without the contaminating tincture of the paternal connection. As one person to another. As one adult with another. When you can converse about matters, and common blood does not color the viewpoints, the conclusions, nor the mode of presentation. When weighty topics can be discussed without being bound by familial ties. Should the use of marijuana be decriminalized? What might be the best posture for the U.S. in the Middle East? Is this stock or that stock the best to buy?

Transcending the parent-child relationship means letting go, but it is a moment to be embraced by both the parent and the child. It is a blessed day when the "never grow up" syndrome (fostered by both children and parents) dissipates; when Peter Pan lies dead; and parents and offspring alike can hold a wake, attend the funeral, and then pitch a party.

Better to "thou" an "it" than
to "it" a "thou," be it a person
or be it a cow.

23 Neither It a Thou nor Thou an It

The eminent Jewish philosopher Martin Buber (1878–1965) published a small volume in 1923 that became one of the most influential books of the twentieth century. Written in German, it was translated into English with the title *I and Thou.*

In this work, written with a mystical flavor, Buber distinguished between two basic types of relations which a person, the "I," can have with other things and people. These are I-It and I-Thou relationships.

In the I-It relationship, the other is treated as an object, as something subject to the needs and purposes of the "I." This is how we relate to most things. Stuff out there—cars, furniture, tools, the environment, and so on—are objects that we use for our convenience and benefit. They are "its."

In "I-Thou" relationships, the "thou" is treated as a full reality in itself and not as a thing or an "it." The "thou" has independent existence as a subject over against the "I." Human relationships are, ideally, always "I-Thou" relationships. The other person is to be regarded as a full individual, who stands over against us with individuality, needs, and rights.

When we treat "thou" relationships as "it" relationships, we turn the "thou" into a thing. Persons are treated as if they were objects to be used for our benefit. We turn people into toys for the games we play. We treat persons as if we were recycling non-biodegradable trash. Workers may be dealt with as if they were merely part of the machinery, cogs in the wheel of production. This depersonalizes persons. This "its a thou."

On the other hand, we can endow an "it" with thouness. In Buber's view, one could have an I-Thou relationship with a special tree or some spot in nature. We can treat a thing as a full subject with its own personality and subjectivity. For most people, an automobile is merely a means of mechanical conveyance that transports their arse and all attached parts from one locale to another. Some people, however, treat their car as a "thou," giving it a name, ascribing it a personality, and even talking to it. This "thous an it," which, of course, is not as destructive as "itting a thou."

Insects and reptiles are generally considered "its." A cockroach, a flea, a fly, a mosquito, and so on is not just an "it," but an it to be hit.

Occupying a region between an "it" and a "thou" are such things as pets and other animals. For some people these are related to as "thous," for others as "its." With ease we step across or slide under the dividing line, if there is one, that separates humans from animals. Probably, if you grieve over something's departure, loss, or death, or if you bury and mark the thing's grave, you are expressing an opinion of the other as a "thou." I've even been accused of treating farm animals as "thous," and it may often be true. I don't object. Better to "thou" an "it" than to "it" a "thou," be it a person or be it a cow.

I raised a bull, "Bully Boy," from a calf knowing he possessed good breeding potential. I indulged him with special care and food. He grew into a marvelous specimen with a high massive neck. A neck a third that size would have been the envy of every NFL lineman. Bully Boy was a gentle creature and a regular pet. He ate from my hand. He jostled to get his share of scratching. Parents photographed their children astride his back.

The bull, however, had one major fault. He firmly believed that every female bovine in the neighborhood was his by necessity and privilege. The seven strands of barbed wire between Bully's kingdom and the neighbor's pasture and herd were only a nuisance not a barrier to him. He considered the neighbor's cows as part of his domain. When Bully invaded, the adjacent bull fled in terror and hid from this hormonal-driven attack machine.

My lectures about proper behavior, territorial boundaries, respect for others' rights, and other topics fell on deaf ears. Bully understood English only when he wanted to and when it didn't subvert his basic drive.

Eventually I was left with only one choice. And I shall never forget the last time our eyes met as he stared through the bars of the trailer hauling him away to the cattle sale. I am sure, had I understood bovine speech, I would have heard him shout: "How could you treat me so long as a THOU and now turn me into an IT? I am a THOU and you know it!" I still bear traitor tracks across my heart.

Turning an "it" into a "thou" is a certain path to greater pain in life. But suffering pain is one of the surest ways to know that you are really alive.

Emeritus looks ahead toward rigor mortis; posthumous has already undergone the experience.

24 Better Emeritus than Posthumous

When professors and others retire or are honorably discharged, they are often awarded the title of "emeritus." Such a position possesses all of the status and none of the rewards of employment. It honors what one has been rather than what one is.

Posthumous, on the other hand, refers to conditions after death. Emeritus looks ahead toward rigor mortis; posthumous has already undergone the experience. In spite of popular etymologizing, the word "posthumous" has nothing to do with *humus*, "dirt" or "earth," as if posthumous referred to a state after decomposition had composted us into a post-humus condition. It is based upon the Latin word *postumus*, "last."

Upon retirement, a professor is often honored with a *Festschrift*, "a festival writing," composed of essays by students and colleagues. A similar work published after one's death is called "a memorial volume." A *Festschrift* is always preferable to a memorial volume, just as emeritus is preferable to posthumous. Receiving commendations is always more fun than receiving commemoration. After all, "a living dog is better than a dead lion" (Ecclesiastes 9:4).

After all, many a hare-brained idea has proven to be right.

25 Chase Rabbits, You Might Scare up an Elephant

When teachers or speakers wander in their lectures and speeches or are prone to dissect minutiae into an infinity of molecules and atoms or are diverted from the topic by some student's or audience member's distracting question, they are said to be "chasing rabbits." On such a chase, teachers and speakers are beyond the subject, beneath the subject, or beside the subject, but never on the subject at hand. Frequently this results in discussing topics that won't be on the exam or even on the subject, however exciting.

For the audience, "chasing rabbits" may create an atmosphere of boredom that, if bottled, could be sold as a cure for the most debilitating case of insomnia. In the battle with boredom, no one stands a chance: "Against boredom even the gods themselves struggle in vain" (Friedrich Wilhelm Nietzsche, 1844–1900; *The Antichrist*, 1888).

Nonetheless, a good word should be said in favor of chasing rabbits, even when we are all alone, thinking or daydreaming. On such forays into the fields and meadows where rabbits romp and play, one may encounter larger game. Topics never before raised, vistas previously unseen, theories yet to be explored, and conclusions heretofore never drawn may lie lurking in the grass and brush. Behind the rabbit's façade or deep within the hare's lair, an elephant may be hidden, waiting to be discovered and aroused. When this happens, the hunt gets interesting. After all, many a hare-brained idea has proven to be right.

Alice found Wonderland chasing after a rabbit. You may too.

Although we should not seek vengeance, nothing prohibits us from witnessing it with a tinge of pleasure.

26   Vengeance is Far too Sweet to Be Enjoyed by the Almighty Alone

In his ethical admonitions in the epistle to the Romans, St. Paul wrote: "Never avenge yourselves but leave room for the wrath of God; for it is written 'Vengeance is mine, I will repay, says the Lord'" (Romans 12:19). As was often the case in antiquity, the writer seems to be quoting from memory. No text in the Hebrew Bible says exactly what Paul claims it does. Deuteronomy 32:35 has God declare: "Vengeance is mine," but lacks the rest of the sentence. Paul may have conjoined in his mind the words of Deuteronomy with Proverbs 20:22:

> Do not say, "I will repay evil";
>> wait for the Lord, and he will help you.

Or maybe Proverbs 24:29:

> Do not say, "I will do to others as they have done to me;
>> I will pay them back for what they have done."

Such sayings as these bring to mind what Christians call the Golden Rule. Jesus is said to have taught: "In everything do to others as you would have them do to you" (Matthew 7:12). This of course calls for fair treatment of the other (unless you happen to be a sadomasochist!). Rabbi Hillel (c. 60 BCE—10 CE) expressed the same idea but in the negative: "What is hateful to you do not do to your neighbor."

These texts do not all clearly rule out human assistance by the wronged party in seeing that the vengeance of the Lord comes about. Nor do they rule out the wronged party's enjoyment of seeing the wrongdoer reap what has been sown. That we can sometimes aid in seeing that justice is done should be of no little consequence and maybe even a sense of delight. A subdued feeling of vengeance can be the icing on the cake of justice. Although we should not seek vengeance, nothing prohibits us from witnessing it with a tinge of pleasure. Rectitude can have its rewards.

Nothing, of course, justifies preemptive vengeance or the principle enunciated by the American novelist, Edward Noyes Westcott (1846–1898): "Do unto the other feller/the way he'd like to do/unto you an' do it first" (*David Harum*, 1898).

We must be immoderate in
our support of moderation,
and refuse to tolerate
intolerance.

27 We Should All be Fanatics for the Cause of Moderation

Most thinking people readily recognize that the radical extremes on any argument, discussion, issue, or practice are generally not the best. Radical right-wing and radical left-wing politics and economics have a record of failure. As Alexander Hamilton (1755–1804) wrote: "Real liberty is neither found in despotism or the extremes of democracy, but in moderate governments" (*Debates of the Federal Convention*, June 16, 1787). Unreasonable spending and scroogian stinginess are both to be eschewed. Gluttony and anorexia both wreak havoc upon the body. Belligerence and timidity are both poor personality traits.

We should all, however, take a do-or-die attitude and fight to the finish for moderation. We should all be extremists against the cause of extremism, intolerant against intolerance. Republican presidential candidate, Barry Goldwater (1909–98), declared in his nomination acceptance speech (July 16, 1964) that "extremism in the defense of liberty is no vice . . . Moderation in the pursuit of justice is no virtue." He lost the election, but maybe he was right about extremism. Thomas Paine (1737–1809) said it a bit differently. "Moderation in temper is always a virtue; but moderation in principle is always a vice" (*The Rights of Man*, Part II).

Whether moderation in principle or practice be a virtue or vice, in our day of extremes, and the rancor they generate, when the middle ground is often no wider than a boundary line, we must be immoderate in our support of moderation, and refuse to tolerate intolerance. When it comes to boiling issues, one cannot afford to be lukewarm.

Today . . . . failure to be suing someone can be taken as lack of social involvement.

28 Speak Softly but Always be Accompanied by a Lawyer with a Big Stick

Speaking at the Minnesota State Fair (September 2, 1901), President Theodore Roosevelt (1858–1919) referred to what he called a homely adage: "Speak softly and carry a big stick; you will go far." He was addressing the issue of the U.S. Navy in relation to the enforcement of the Monroe Doctrine.

Today we live in a litigious society where everyone wants to use a stick. The failure to be suing someone can be taken as lack of social involvement, evidence of being an anti-cultural misfit, proof of being out of tune with the times. Not to assume a victim status seems immoral, perhaps arrogant, or at least weak. We have reached the stage where blaming someone else seems to free us from personal reproach and responsibility. Why assume the credit for your own mistakes and misery when others can be blamed?

We no longer heed the advice offered centuries ago by the British theologian and poet, George Herbert (1593–1633): "Go not for every grief to the physician, nor for every quarrel to the lawyer, nor for every thirst to the pot" (*Jacula Prudentum*, 1651). Perhaps we now allow our common instincts to control our behavior: "The masters have been done away with; the morality of the common man has triumphed" (Friedrich Wilhelm Nietzsche, 1844–1900; *Beyond Good and Evil*, 1885–1886). Our inherited primordial evolutionary drive to lash out and to strike back is no longer controlled by the restraining hand of civility.

Our suing society is encouraged by and supports a mammoth industry, the legal profession. Lawyers, however, belong to a long, honorable, and perhaps falsely maligned profession. Nearly three hundred years ago Benjamin Franklin (1706–90), who wasn't one, could speak of lawyers in the following terms: "God works wonders now and then;

Behold! A lawyer, an honest man" (*Poor Richard's Almanac*, 1733). Members of the legal profession, like those of other helping professions, are sometime tempted, like frenzied, feeding maggots, to grow fat off the pus of human misery.

In today's world, where you can't carry a big stick, you had best have a lawyer on call.

All of these are ways we demonstrate that our life has been more than a dash between two dates on a headstone.

29 Try to Bequeath Your Children More Than a Copy of Your Bankruptcy Statement

Society has long debated the virtues and vices of inheritance laws. Should one generation be encouraged or even allowed to transfer to the next the gains it has amassed? Is it beneficial to the inheritors and society as a whole for the next to feed upon a largess from the last? Only the most radical of liberals, however, would claim that we should forego all inheritance.

Numerous arguments on the issue of inheritance abound. Individuals should be required to accomplish their own success, so some argue. Everyone should have to start on a level playing field. Even to assume a level playing field exists is nonsense, their opponents declare. The benefits of the past are the property of the past to be employed as those of the past may chose.

Doubts about inheritant benefits were already alive in antiquity. The ancient Hebrew skeptic who wrote the book of Ecclesiastes declared: "I must leave it to those who come after me—and who knows whether they will be wise or foolish? Yet they will be master of all for which I toiled and used my wisdom under the sun. This also is vanity" (Ecclesiastes 2:18–19).

Whether we like it or not, what we leave our children in the way of finances says something about how we have lived. How we have spent what we had, how we have used what we had, how much we have given away of what we had—these all speak volumes too. All of these are ways we demonstrate that our life has been more than a dash between two dates on a headstone. Parents who burn the economic candle at both ends often leave the children only the smoke of a smoldering wick. Such parents spend their final years living on their memories and off Medicare and their Social Security checks, unless, of course, the children pitch in and become parent redeemers.

Many a parent dies leaving behind only the shell of the life that might have been—and a legacy of squandering. Nobody, however, ever frames and displays a bankruptcy statement.

Personas, like the stage masks from which the name derives, are partially artificial but entirely necessary in the drama of life.

30 Some of the Time Some of Us Have Two Faces, but All of the Time All of Us Have Four Personas

A two-faced person is one considered deceitful and hypocritical, pretending one thing while knowingly being another. Most of us are this way sometimes, putting forth one face while trying to save the other. Duplicity and questionable integrity are the price we pay for ego preservation.

In reality, behind our faces, we all are four different persons, four different personas, four divergent personalities. Personas, like the stage masks from which the name derives, are partially artificial but entirely necessary in the drama of life.

There is, first, our public persona. This is the personality we project, or attempt to project, to others. Often, it is manicured, polished, and practiced; after all we like to put our "best face" forward. This public persona provides the raw material for what others come to expect of us; what others use in calculating our anticipated behavior and assessing our past activity.

We are all aware that the fabric of our public persona is interlaced with threads of fakery and fraud, pretence, and prefabrication. Only the foolish and the egomaniacal would assume that their public persona is their real self. One of the surest ways to self-incineration is to operate on such a hypothesis. The only thing more pathetic than believing your public persona is your real persona is for someone else to believe it about you.

Secondly, there is the persona we believe ourselves to be. We all know that our public persona contains a limited amount of pretense and an unlimited amount of makeup. Nonetheless, we have a self-image of our personality, of who we are. Are we honest? Truthful? Deceptive?

Calculating? How do we react in crisis? How do we respond to temptation? Are we morally good? Do we act on the basis of a moral compass? And so forth. We are a certain way because that is how persons like we believe ourselves to be are expected to act. Our self-perception provides us with images of character and actions and establishes patterns and boundaries for our behavior. A spouse, loyal to the marriage vows, is not only being faithful to the partner but also to their self-image as a person who lives up to their promises and covenant obligations. Such a one knows that you do not give your life to another with expectations of reclaiming it someday amid the bumps along the road of life.

Rosa Parks, on December 1, 1955, in Montgomery, Alabama, refused to get up and vacate her seat on a public bus and move to the back so her seat could be occupied by a person privileged by both custom and law, that is, so it could be occupied by a greasy slab of fat, white ass. When she did this, she was probably acting on the basis of her self-understanding, her self-image: a person deserving rights, a full human personality sharing an equality with her white, fellow passengers for whom any seat on the bus was purchased with merely the price of a ticket and requiring no genealogical pedigree. She knew she was not some animal to be herded to the rear and corralled like a domesticated sub-human species.

Thirdly, there is the persona we really are. This is the person we are when there is no public to impress and no necessary self-standards to be met. Sometimes this is called the secret self, but it is the self as it finds expression when there are no restraining boundaries and no weighty pressures of peer or even self-evaluation. The driver in heavy, anonymous traffic, for example, tends to express the real self—often to the embarrassment of the believed self. When our inhibitions are closeted and the moment is ripe, our true self can unexpectedly horrify us, like a werewolf on a moonless night. Many in their sobriety have confronted the reality of *in vino veritas*.

Fourthly, there is, for lack of a better expression, the submerged self, the self that lurks beneath the membrane separating the conscious and the unconscious. Alligators and crocodiles slither through the swamps of our unconscious waiting to shred and consume our best intentions and to mutilate our noblest aspirations.

Here are the forces that turn us into the miserable little bastards we so often become. Within these swamps lie the surds of our evolutionary past; the unextinquished, smoldering ashes of our suppressed natural inclinations; the psychological junk produced by how we have been handled and how we have handled ourselves; the shriveled, shivering fears that corrode the edges of our every appearance of confidence and security; and enough demons to populate an enormous Halloween party. But here also are those drives, inclinations, and embodiments that can propel us to the unexpected and sometimes even to the valiant. In our unconscious sprout the seeds of both cruelty and kindness.

Within the swamps of our unconscious there are also to be found long-legged, pink-hued flamingoes adding color and beauty to life; eagles that can soar through space and whose eyes can provide us with vistas unimagined; plants whose fragrances can ignite in us images long dormant and memories with contours long faded into oblivion; and refreshing waters whose sources forever remain unknown and unseen. Our submerged self, and all its panoramas, finds expression in our dreams and in our spontaneous acts heroic and psychotic, when we do and are what neither others nor ourselves would ever have expected. "The unconscious is not just evil by nature, it is also the source of the highest good; not only dark but also light, not only bestial, semi-human, and demonic but superhuman, spiritual . . ." (Carl Jung, 1875–1961; *The Practice of Psychotherapy*, 1953).

The melding of all four personas into one is impossible and probably not even desirable. Instead, be all four, unashamedly, and "know thyselves." And hope and pray that the four coexist with a modicum of harmony.

You yourself are often your best conversation partner.

31 A Book of Verses, a Jug of Wine, a Loaf of Bread, and Who Needs a Thou

The English poet, Edward Fitzgerald (1809–1883), first translated the *Rubáiyát* of the Persian Omar Khayyám (died about 1133) in 1859. One of its sections reads:

> A Book of Verses underneath the Bough,
> A Jug of Wine, a Loaf of Bread—and Thou
> Beside me singing in the Wilderness—
> Oh, Wilderness were Paradise enow! (stanza 12)

This passage celebrates being alone together—isolation with companionship.

Isolation without companionship, that is, solitude, has not always had a good press. Even the opening passages of the book of Genesis have God declare to the heavenly beings: "It is not good that the man (Adam) should be alone; I will make him a helper as his partner" (Genesis 2:18). The Roman Stoic philosopher, Seneca (4 BCE—65 CE) believed that "solitude prompts us to all kinds of evil."

Some have simultaneously both lauded and deprecated solitude:

> I praise the Frenchman, his remark was shrewd—
> "How sweet, how passing sweet is solitude."
> But grant me still a friend in my retreat,
> To whom I may whisper—Solitude is sweet.
> —William Cowper (1731–1800, *Retirement*)

Others have openly praised solitude, the state of aloneness. Solitude provides the conditions for self-awareness, for self-analysis (a primary function of prayer), for time alone with the one who knows you best, for self-criticism, for self-encouragement, for self-conversation, for self-isolation, and for self-renewal: "far from the madding crowd's ignoble strife" (Thomas Gray, 1716–1771; *Elegy*

Written in a Country Churchyard, 1750). You, yourself, are, after all, your best therapist.

The philosopher, Ayn Rand (1905–1982), wrote: "Civilization is the progress toward a society of privacy. The savage's whole existence is public, ruled by the laws of the tribe. Civilization is the process of setting man free from men" (*The Fountainhead*, 1943). Rainer Maria Rilke (1875–1926) even wrote: "A good marriage is that in which each appoints the other guardian of his solitude" (*Letters*). Lord Byron (1788–1824) wrote that "solitude should teach us how to die" (*Childe Harold's Pilgrimage* IV, 1818) since dying itself is the ultimate aloneness.

The individual who, in school or on one's own, has learned how to learn, how to think, how to explore the inner self, can be their own best company. In introspection, one can engage philosophy, theology, music, psychology, and a host of other matters, and discover that you yourself are often your best conversation partner. In solitude you can delve into the deep and often troubling waters of your self-perception. Memories can flood our minds, be ingested anew and digested afresh, revealing morsels of insight previously unsuspected. Detachment provides the occasion for regeneration and rejuvenation. In our solitude, we can experience such dreams as stuff is made of.

Omar Khayyám recommended a book, wine, bread, and a thou. A book of verse provides raw material for thought, insight, and inspiration, for mental activity. Wine perforates the barriers in the mind and opens the cockles in the heart. Bread sustains the body and fills the belly. But is there a need for a thou? Isolation and solitude help us make companions of ourselves.

The crushed heart . . . long soaked in tears of pain and sorrow becomes impervious to restoration.

32 The Heart That Has Been Broken Can Be Mended; The Heart That Has Been Crushed Can Never Be Repaired

The heart is not by nature a fragile organ. It already sustains the life of the fetus within the mother's womb. In a normal person it beats about 70 times a minute, 4200 times an hour, 100,800 times a day, 36,792,000 times a year, and 2,943,360,000 times during an eighty-year life span.

In the ancient world, the heart was considered the center of the intellect and will. "As a person thinks in the heart, so is one" (Proverbs 23:7). (A remnant of this way of thinking is preserved until today: in the expression "to learn something by heart.") In negotiating, the ancients spoke to the heart and when a negotiator was satisfied, the matter was "pleasing to the heart," that is, agreed upon, settled.

In modern metaphorical speech, language of the heart is closely related to romance, passion, and commitment. (The stylized heart that adorns our modern valentines was most likely originally not intended as a heart, but as a stylized view from the rear of a person bent over from the waist.) In matters of love and commitment, we speak of winning someone's heart, giving one's heart, breaking one's heart, and so on.

Some actions break the heart; others crush it. A promise made but a promise unkept may break the heart; many promises made but unkept may crush the heart. Habituation forecloses healing. A single sexual liaison, the product of a chance meeting or some accidental encounter, when one succumbs to old-fashion passion, may break a partner's heart. Cold, calculated, and repeated acts of infidelity crush the heart. The former is a consequence of coincidence; the latter the result of plot and scheme. One incident of disrespect may break the heart. A pattern of persistent disrespect crushes the heart.

A broken heart, an injured heart, preserves its integrity, its capacity to respond, and its ability to revive in hope. Gentle care, affective attention, and tender regard can coax the wounded heart to health even if they cannot erase the scars. "A wounded heart can with difficulty be cured" (Johann Wolfgang von Goethe, 1749–1832; *Torquato Tasso*, 1790).

The crushed heart, however, long soaked in tears of pain and sorrow becomes impervious to restoration. Tear-moistened it may simply solidify and turn to concrete, impenetrable stuff, never again to experience tenderness and affection. "My heart is turned to stone; I strike it and it hurts my hand" (Shakespeare, *Othello*). Or the crushed heart may liquefy, lacking the fiber and cohesion to respond to love ever again.

> As an egg, when broken, never
> Can be mended, but must ever
> Be the same crushed egg for ever—
> So shall this dark heart of mine.
> —T. H. Chivers (1809–1858, *To Allegra Florence in Heaven*)

Energies are better spent on appreciating and enhancing the everyday than trying to turn every day into a holiday.

33   Develop a Capacity to Glorify the Routine

President Abraham Lincoln (1809–1865) is said to have declared that "common-looking people are the best in the world: that is the reason God makes so many of them" (reported in the diary of John Hay, December 23, 1863). God must also love the routine, since our lives are so packed full of it.

The writer of the biblical book of Ecclesiastes lamented the common routine, the monotony of existence, uncertain whether life was just one damn thing after another or whether it was the same damn thing over and over and over again.

For many, life consists in being daily served the same sandwich over and over and over again. We are propelled along on a sea of routine, wearisome regularity: the same job, the same duties, the same problems, the same schedule, the same house, the same spouse, the same family, the same meals, the same scenery, and on and on and on.

Most of life is about as exciting as watching a PBS volunteer answering the phone during fundraising week. Frequently life encounters us as sixty minutiae per hour. Existence can seem like a tomb with both ends kicked out. We all sometimes experience that "inexorable boredom that is at the core of life" (Jacques Bénigne Bossuet, 1627–1704).

For the ancients, life was even more monotonous than for us. Most, throughout their lives, resided in the same village, among the same few hundred persons; never traveled more than a few miles from home; went to bed at dusk; rose at dawn; labored in the same small fields every day; ate their way through the year on whatever was seasonal and available; and were finally buried in the family tomb containing dozens of relatives' skeletons. Even war could be greeted as a welcome change of pace!

Mark Twain (1835–1910) has Tom Sawyer give expression to the routinization of life: "She makes me wash, they comb me all to thunder; she won't let me sleep in the woodshed . . . the wider eats by a bell; she goes to bed by a bell; she gits up by a bell—everything's so awful reg'lar a body can't stand it" (*The Adventures of Tom Sawyer*, 1876).

> What has been is what will be,
>   and what has been done is what will be done;
> there is nothing new under the sun.
>   (Ecclesiastes 1:9)

One of the secrets to a contented life, however, is learning how to appreciate that routine (while maybe occasionally sleeping in the woodshed!). Persons who have undergone a near death experience and then found an unexpected lease on life speak of their new ability to savor the ordinary things in everyday experience. Many told they have a terminal illness quickly learn to cherish the normal. So do troops returning home from some foreign military expedition. For them the ordinary has clothed itself in the extraordinary. Life would be more pleasing, pleasurable, and meaningful if we could all do the same. Energies are better spent on appreciating and enhancing the everyday than trying to turn every day into a holiday.

A thin vein of gold threads itself through everything ordinary and routine; recognizing that fact and learning how to mine it are important clues to finding happiness in life. The humdrum always forms the skeleton of all our fondest memories. Paradoxically, our deepest emotions and our strongest passions are embodied in what can appear as the most superficial of our actions and relationships. Our deepest affections are not expressed in those moments of extreme passion and intensity but in the normal routines of everyday existence.

Learn to romance the routine and to find the romantic in the eternally repeated every day. Viewed through the proper prism, the modest and the mundane can appear as the magnificent. Often, boredom can be absolutely beautiful. Amid the normalities of the routine, the attentive can occasionally seem to feel the brush of angelic wings.

Could anything be more optimistic than hoping we will spend our final hours performing the normalties of life, reenacting the rituals of routine?

The French philosopher/essayist Montaigne (1533–92) wrote: "I want death to find me planting my cabbages" (*Essays*, I, 20). One can hope to die in the harness.

Sometimes, when you sense yourself well and truly bored, thank your higher power that life is so damned routine, regular, and ordinary. The opposite could be disastrous.

Punishment itself, applied from the outside, seldom if ever rejuvenates and redirects the internal will.

34 When Someone Sets Out to Rehabilitate You, Run Like a Scalded Dog

For many generations, most tort and non-capital criminal law was focused on the victim, not the perpetrator. The goal was to restore the victim, as nearly as possible, to the condition existing prior to the wrongdoing. Biblical texts illustrate this approach (see Leviticus 6:1–7 [5:20–27 in Jewish Bibles]; Numbers 5:5–10). The wrongdoer, out of remorse and regret, offered confession and paid or restored the principal involved to the wronged party plus a penalty of twenty percent. With public acknowledgment and restitution of the injured—confession with accountability— the matter was over. Normalcy had been restored.

Somewhere along the line, probably influenced by the Christian doctrine of redemption, the focus shifted from the victim to the wrongdoer. Rehabilitation of the criminal replaced restitution for the victim. The goal was to change the wrongdoer, to save the sinner. Prisons began to flourish. Punishment became widespread.

Efforts at enforced rehabilitation have generally been a failure. Prisons often don't rehabilitate the wrongdoer but merely intensify the criminal drive. The Irish playwright and poet Oscar Wilde (1854–1900) wrote of prisons:

> The vilest deeds like poison weeds
> Bloom well in prison air:
> It is only what is good in man
> That wastes and withers there:
> Pale anguish keeps the heavy gate
> And the warden is Despair.
> (*The Ballad of Reading Gaol*, 1898)

Punishment itself, applied from the outside, seldom if ever rejuvenates and redirects the internal will. The American educator Horace Mann (1796–1859) wrote: "The object of punishment is prevention from evil; it never can be made impulsive to good" (*Lectures and Reports on Education*, 1866).

Rehabilitation attempts, externally imposed with the purpose to redeem and re-do someone else, practically never succeed. Only when the move to rehabilitate is met and embraced by an internal drive to change is there hope. The internal move must take priority over the external movement. When one recognizes one's own need for help, the race should be not from, but to the rehabilitator.

Sometimes it is better to admit that things didn't work out, and probably won't and even couldn't work out, than to hang on to an empty hope.

35   Avoid Having to Pay Alimony on Your Alimony Payments

I have been married and divorced three times—each time to and from the same woman. (All my three children were by my first wife.) Maybe I chose to marry her consecutively because in elementary school I had been taught that "if you don't get it right the first time, do it again." In the second and third weddings, I didn't have to say "I do," but rather, "I already did." I had to give up when the "three strikes and you are out" law was passed.

Why the repetition? Perhaps we were just addicted to each other. Perhaps the embers of love never went out. Perhaps somewhere in the deep recesses of my heart, affection still occupied a small apartment. Perhaps the expectation of an unrealizable intimacy remained as a hopeful fantasy. Perhaps my life was being choreographed by a very stupid Cupid. Perhaps familiarity had bred an ease of mind. Perhaps existence in a bad situation appeared preferable to the unknown, since a known bad certainty seems better than any unknown uncertainty. Perhaps we both thought it best to dance with the devil you know. Perhaps I expected that another camera would get better pictures even when photographing the same terrain. Perhaps my hope, like plants, grew best where the compost was deepest. Perhaps people are even more stupid than we give them credit for.

I could argue that some advantages accrued from remarrying the same woman. You always had the same mother-in-law. There were never any great surprises on the honeymoon. The monogrammed towels didn't need changing. Better the same mare then a new mustang to tame. There was the convenience of introducing only one woman as your ex-wives.

Every time matters got more costly. Expensive counseling sessions. Extravagant lawyer fees. And alimony. Alimony on the alimony.

Sometimes it is better to admit that things didn't work out, and probably won't and even couldn't work out, than to hang on to an empty hope. Nothing is to be gained from standing ankle deep in the ashes, trying to figure out what sparked the incineration. Cut the costs, express regrets, bid adieu, flee the scene, shed the tears, and fight the depression. Occasionally, all's well that ends.

A dog learns not to jump from a moving car by jumping from a moving car.

36 The Highest Tuition is Always Charged on Lessons Already Learned

Proverbs are short sayings based on long experience. They are "the wisdom of the many and the wit of the one." The wisdom they encapsulate is best understood looking backward or looking upward. After the horse has been stolen even the stupid will shut the stable door. Lying in a ditch, you understand why you should look before you leap. The recent divorcee can comprehend, "marry in haste, repent at leisure." Even animals are the same way. A dog learns not to jump from a moving car by jumping from a moving car. All of us make mistakes and none of us was born a pencil, with a large eraser for removing missteps and errors. Experience is the name we give to our mistakes.

As long ago as the Greek poet Homer (about 700 BCE), people already knew that our experience and especially our mistakes are great teachers: "a fool . . . sees the mischiefs that are past" (Homer, *Iliad*); "the event is the schoolmaster of fools" (Livy, 59 BCE—17 CE, *History*).

The cost of our mistakes can be enormous; it is always collected with interest. A wrong turn taken, an impulse ignored, (or followed, of course, depending on the outcome), a vicious thought spoken, an urge acted upon, care forgotten, the wrong nut turned, the computer disk unbackedup, a map wrongly read, directions not followed, poor business deals, greed that grasps at a scam—these and more are the driving engines of our mistake mobile.

Many of our mistakes are the consequence of a failure of thought and reflection, although poor and stupid processes up front can sometime produce as bad results down the road as no processes at all. Stupid things we do are hard or impossible to head off and drive back into the barn. Perhaps the philosopher, René Descartes (1596–1650) should not have said, "I think therefore I am" but rather "I think therefore I won't." Many people spend a lifetime having to harvest bitter fruit from the trees of their poor judgments and wrong decisions. When in doubt, don't.

The American novelist John Updike (1932–2009) has written: "A healthy male adult consumes each year one and a half times his own weight in other people's patience" (*Assorted Prose*, 1965). Our mistakes wear out other people. We pay, and others have to grant us scholarships in order to pick up part of our tuition.

The mistakes we commit nearly always involve us in explanation. Few follow the advice of John Arbuthnot Fisher (1841–1920) who, in a letter to the *Times of London* (September 5, 1919), wrote: "Never contradict. Never explain. Never apologize. (These are the secrets of a happy life!)." In the screenplay for *She Wore a Yellow Ribbon* (1949), one character declares, "Never apologize and never explain—it's a sign of weakness." Weakness or not, we all want to explain our mistakes to ourselves. Explanation provides at least the expectation of illumination. With regard to others, apology seeks to undo what cannot be changed. When it comes to explanation, we ought to remember that "an ounce of forethought is worth a pound of apology." In metric terms, that is "28.35 grams of forethought is worth 454.5 grams of apology."

Mistakes are the potholes in the highway of experience. We ought to learn from them and profit from the tuition paid.

If that one was "good," what might the others be?

37 Beware of Adjectival Denigration, or, There Never Was a "Good" Samaritan

The expression "a good Samaritan" is almost universally used and understood even by those completely unaware of its origin. We employ it in reference to someone who performs kind and unselfish acts of generosity or philanthropy.

The expression derives from a story told by Jesus, reported only in the Gospel of Luke (Luke 10:25–37). According to the story, a man, on the road from Jerusalem to Jericho, was robbed, beaten, and left half-dead. Religious leaders passed by without offering help. Finally he was rescued and cared for by someone else passing that way. This helper was a Samaritan. The Samaritans, who still survive in minuscule number in the state of Israel, were a deviant Jewish sect, which claimed Mt. Gerizim near Shechem as the sacred mountain of God, not Mt. Zion in Jerusalem. Other Jews considered them a heterodox, half-breed community.

In the biblical story, the Samaritan is never called "good." This has been added in the course of history. The use of the adjective, however, has serious consequences for understanding the story. There is a world of difference between "a Samaritan performed an act of mercy" and the "good Samaritan performed an act of mercy." The latter implies that the rest of the Samaritans, or at least a majority, were not "good." This is adjectival denigration.

When we say a "good" anyone (Samaritan, Black, Muslim, Christian, or whatever) did such and such, it casts a shadow of doubt and suspicion over everyone else in the same class. If that one was "good," what might the others be? Our adjectives reflect our evaluations and attitudes. As the English poet and lexicographer Samuel Johnson (1709–1784) said: "Don't attitudinize" (James Boswell, *Life of Johnson*, 1791).

Regardless of our frills, toys, jewels, and gidgits and gadgets, we, too, are what we are.

38 In Spite of Added Frills, a Bathroom is Still a Toilet

Anyone tempted by an overly exalted view of the nobility of humankind should spend a few minutes in an old-fashioned, well-used outhouse. The earthiness of humanity, aerially and aromatically borne, that would gag a skunk, will immediately demythologize one's view.

These often square outbuildings with crescent-shaped light sources used to adorn every backyard, monuments erected to human necessity. They ranged from one to three seaters, that is, one to three holers. Multiplicity in usage, however, was generally the exception. One didn't desire company when doing one's business unless the emergency was dire.

In the summertime, the outhouse was baked in the burning sun and could get as hot as an August day in Hades. In the wintertime, placing your unclothed bottom on a cold wooden board could produce temporary mental paralysis, leaving you uncertain about why you were there in the first place.

Wasps were frequent co-inhabitors of outhouses, often constructing their nests not only in the corners of the building but also beneath the hole-bearing boards. In early spring, one was constantly serenaded by the music of bumblebees gnawing out their tunnels in any portion of wood thick enough to provide them refuge. The wasps' and bees' uncertain location could add a certain excitement to the daily routine. For years, the majority of black-widow spider bites were on the posterior of outhouse habituates.

The passage of time, the invention of electric pumps, and the use of piped water led to the placement of toilets inside homes and buildings. Once inside the house, the toilet and its basic function joined company with those mechanisms attendant upon bathing. People were not content with merely a water closet. The toilet precinct evolved into the bathroom.

Gradually, the bathroom became one of the more elaborately furnished rooms in a home. Much was added to disguise its fundamental role and to camouflage its service to one of humanity's basic needs. Gradually it became so large, lavish, and luxurious that the British critic, Edmund Wilson (1895–1972), could write:

> I have had a good many more uplifting thoughts, creative and expansive visions—while soaking in comfortable baths or drying myself after bracing showers—in well-equipped American bathrooms than I have ever had in any cathedral. (*A Piece of My Mind*, 1956)

When stripped of its frills, the bathroom's fundamental character nonetheless remains the same, always exuding its connection with its old forerunner. Even in Buckingham Palace, with its royally appointed furnishings, the Queen, we presume, still stinks up the bathroom, demonstrating that even royalty shares features of our common humanity; even uncommoners share facets of life with the commoners.

Like bathrooms, regardless of our frills, toys, jewels, and gidgits and gadgets, we, too, are what we are.

If we eat meat we should
always consume it . . .
knowing that something lost
its life for us.

39 If You Couldn't Kill It, You Shouldn't Eat It

Human diets and animal rights have become interwoven in contemporary conversation. Vegetarianism has ceased to be merely a topic of general discussion and the habit of a few but has become a way of life for the many. The old issue of the treatment of animals no longer centers merely around the subject of hunting as a sport but with mass production of meat for consumption it has become an issue for the masses.

As long ago as the Latin poet, Ovid (43 BCE—18 CE), a case was made against killing and eating animals. He wrote:

> Oh, how criminal it is for flesh to be stored away in flesh, for one greedy body to grow fat with food gained from another, for one live creature to go on living through the destruction of another living thing! And so in the midst of the wealth of food which earth, the best of mothers, has produced, it is your pleasure to chew the piteous flesh of slaughtered animals! (*Metamorphoses*)

Long before Ovid penned these words, the priestly author of material in the opening chapters of the Book of Genesis presented the ten generations from Adam to Noah as vegetarian. Only after the flood were humans granted the right to kill and eat flesh (see Genesis 9:1–7).

The multigenius Leonardo da Vinci (1452–1519) wrote in *The Notebooks* (1508–1518): "Man and the animals are merely a passage and channel for food, a tomb for other animals, a haven for the dead, giving life by the death of others, a coffer full of corruption."

Eating meat always involves killing. Hunting has long had to be defended as a rational and sensible means of killing. When hunting supplied the table, of course, no question was asked. Humans could give vent productively to a natural inclination: "There is a passion for hunting something deeply implanted in the human heart" (Charles Dickens, 1812–1870; *Oliver Twist*, 1837–1838). In recent years, society has slept uneasily with hunting merely for sport: "When man wants to murder a tiger he calls it sport: When the tiger wants to murder him he calls it ferocity" (George Bernard Shaw, 1856–1950, *Maxims for Revolutionists*). For hunters, killing may be a sport; for the hunted animal it is the finale. The English poet, Walter de la Mare (1873–1956), has rhythmically expressed the point:

> Bang! Now the animal
> Is dead and dumb and done.
> Nevermore to peep again, creep again, leap again,
> Eat or sleep or drink again, oh, what fun!

It has been presumed that killing animals stimulates the urge to kill humans: "The urge to kill, like the urge to beget, is blind and sinister. Its craving is set today on the flesh of a hare: Tomorrow it can howl the same way for the flesh of a man" (Andrei Andreevich Voznesenski, 1953–; *Hunting a Hare*, 1964). This position, however, is questionable. Many hunters are very humane and compassionate ecologists and environmentalists, and certainly not murderers. For centuries, humans in the pursuit of food hunted by the rules, "if you can't eat it, you shouldn't kill it" and "if you killed it, you eat it." Many meat-eaters today, however, take no thought for the source of their food as if meat were produced painlessly and grown to maturity in sanitized, plastic wrapping.

More respect might be paid the costs of our feasting if names were not changed between the farm and the restaurant menu: if we listed not pork but "pig flesh," not beef but "cow flesh," not mutton but "sheep flesh." "Hamburger" could be called "ground dead cow." Maybe we should have some means to require that all meat eaters demonstrate that they could slaughter before they consume. One should not only pick the lobster but also have to drop it into a pot of boiling water. Maybe we should wring a chicken's neck before sinking our teeth into a chicken salad sandwich.

At any rate, if we eat meat we should always consume it with a tinge of regret and remorse, even with a bit of reverence, knowing that something lost its life for us.

The role of prepositions
in languages highlights
the importance of the little
things in life.

40 The Meaning is Always in the Prepositions

The dictionary defines a preposition as "a class of words that are used before nouns or adjectives to form phrases functioning as modifiers of verbs, nouns, or adjectives, and that express a spatial, temporal, or other relationship." In layman's language, they are those little particles that we are not supposed to end a sentence with. Modern-day speech now generally ignores the fact that prepositions should precede rather than follow. The most notorious preposition-ending sentence is a child's protest about being read a bedtime story from a book about Australia: "Why did you bring that book which I don't want to be read to out of from about 'Down Under' up for?"

The role of prepositions in languages highlights the importance of the little things in life. If one takes the simple verb "to act," whose general meaning is clear, and adds prepositions, a whole new gamut of meanings becomes present: "to act out," "to act on," "to act up." Or the verb "to eat": "to eat up," "to eat in," "to eat out." Not to speak of the old problem of whether a house "burns up" or "burns down" or takes the simple way out and just "burns." Sometimes a preposition completely alters the meaning of a verb: "to bless" versus "to bless out." "To bless" is to bestow a benefit or the promise and wish of a benefit upon another. It always carries positive connotations. "To bless out" means to condemn, accuse, denounce. It always carries negative connotations. One "blessed" walks with head held high, anticipating the best. One "blessed out" tucks tail between the legs and slinks away.

The prepositions "out," "up," and "in" make all the difference in the meaning of the verb "to give." "To give out" denotes exhaustion, you have no more to give. Your game is over, at least temporarily. "To give up" denotes surrender. You have chosen to exert or fight no longer. The white flag becomes the symbol of the moment. "To give in" may seem to mean the same as "to give up." But such is not the case. Giving in may mean one has chosen to be defeated rather than destroyed. A head bowed in submission need not be a head bowed in surrender as slaves and the oppressed have known throughout history. Giving in can be a time for reloading, for restrategizing, a time to look forward to better times and maybe even ultimate success and victory. Confronting an overwhelming crisis or arms too strong to oppose requires us to decide whether "giving up" or "giving in" is the better policy. Knowing the difference can be a determinative factor in the long-range outcome. Jesus advised his followers to be as harmless as a dove but as wise as a snake (see Matthew 10:16). Surely he included knowing when to give in and when to give up.

Like a thousand other little things in life, prepositions have their important roles to play and can be ignored only with disastrous consequences.

We delight in the surge
of adrenalin that rushes
through our veins when we
escape over the walls of our
commitments.

41 A Mangy Dog Will Let Anybody Scratch It

Canines are especially susceptible to sarcoptic mange produced by infinitesimally small mites. These parasites attack the host and produce itching frenzies. The dog, seeking to relieve the itch, may scratch itself furiously. Obviously, having something else, like a human, do the scratching can be an absolute delight. It has even been argued that every dog needs a reason to scratch: a touch of mange or a few fleas: "A reasonable amount o'fleas is good fer a dog—keeps him from broodin' over *bein'* a dog" (American novelist, Edward Noyes Westcott, 1847–1898; *David Harum*, 1898). What other purpose do fleas serve, anyway? The poor dog, when heavily infested, will seek out and allow anyone to scratch it. It will scrub its back on bushes and anything that offers a rubbing surface.

Like dogs, people too can become mangy with real or imagined needs. To overcome the itch they will allow anyone to scratch them. Whole communities and nations may give themselves over to despots and totalitarian regimes who promise to handle the itch. People with the mange will submit to having no place to go so long as the trains run on time. Votes can be obtained with a promise to provide a scratching post.

Mange does not have to be real to send one into a scratching frenzy. Imaginary mange is probably more widespread than the genuine article. It is no accident that we speak of the seven-year itch, a phrase made popular by the 1952 play with the same name by the American director and playwright, George Axelrod (1922–2003). It is that time in a marriage when imaginary mange becomes epidemic and experimenting, straying, and exploring become common.

Rather than spending five percent of our time wondering how we got where we are and ninety-five percent of the time making the most of the present situation, we reverse the figures. Our kicking against the pricks is transformed into grand designs of great escape. We itch to switch from our personal ditch. We cut loose the past, we mortgage the present, and we place all our expectations on the future. We yearn to be served a bowl of ecstasy to supplement our diet of constant monotony (and monogamy).

For some, a new job or a new career seems to offer a scratch exactly where the itch is the most concentrated. So we gamble; we take risks. For others, some new adventure promises to restore our youth, to return us to the time when the itch did not yet plague us. The itch drives us to look for a new spouse or a new lover or a new lover who is not a spouse, at least not our own. We search for someone to rescue us from the routine, to provide us with glibly spoken words we do not daily hear. Hot air panted by someone unfamiliar seems far more preferable than the air we breathe with our old familiars. Sneaked sugar always seems to taste sweeter. We delight in the surge of adrenalin that rushes through our veins when we escape over the walls of our commitments. So we become infected and debilitated by severe cases of adulteritis. The mange pushes us to sacrifice what should be permanent and priceless on the cheap and fleeting altar of the momentary. The mange can lead us to produce strings of entanglements that can become a web entrapping us, to await the bite of the spider of our own creation.

We can easily become a slave to our itches. Frequently others can convince us that we have an itch even when we have hardly thought about making a scratch. The whole advertising business operates on such a postulate, as do tempters of all shades and stripes.

A dog's mange is not cured but only worsened by the scratching. One removes the itch by attacking and treating the mites; the sooner the better. So with humans, and imaginary mange: "It is easier to resist at the beginning than at the end" (Leonardo da Vinci, 1452–1519, *The Notebooks*, 1508–1518).

Was it merely coincidental that an Old Middle English and Icelandic expression used to refer to the devil was "Old Scratch"?

Only a cadaver should
receive nothing but
compliments.

42 Cheap Compliments Are Seldom Worth Their Price

Some people fit into the category of superlativists. They never saw or met anything or anybody about which they couldn't offer highest praise and exalted compliment. "Ah, that is such a lovely wart on the end of your nose!" they would have said to Marcus Tullius (106–43 BCE), who bore the nickname Cicero ("chick pea") because of the huge, pea-sized protuberance that adorned his snout.

Throughout the centuries, thinkers have warned against both the giving and the receiving of compliments, suspecting that praise always has its price. Thus François, Duc de La Rochefoucauld (1613–1680): "Usually we praise only to be praised"; "the gratitude of most men is merely a secret desire to receive greater benefits" (*Reflections; or, Sentences and Moral Maxims*, 1678, maxims 146 and 298). American humorist, Josh Billings (Henry Wheeler Shaw, 1818–1885), declared that "flattery is like Kolone water, tew be smelt of, not swallowed" (*Philosophy*).

Those who offer cheap compliments are in reality more harmful than helpful. The Roman historian Tacitus (about 55 CE—about 117 CE) spoke of "those worst of enemies, flatterers" (*Agricola*). The English poet and dramatist George Chapman (about 1559—about 1634) said it even better: "Flatterers look like friends, as wolves, like dogs" (*The Conspiracy of Charles, Duke of Baron*, 1608). Those whose egos must be buoyed by the hot air of cheap compliments are like flies that live off methane-laded manure. "Flattery corrupts both the receiver and the giver" (English statesman, Edmund Burke, 1729–1797; *Reflections of the Revolution in France*, 1790).

The French playwright, Molière (1622–1673), advised that "the more we love our friends, the less we flatter them; it is by excusing nothing that pure love shows itself" (*Le Misanthrope*, 1666). If something "nice" is all someone can

say about or to us, pray that they will hold their tongues
and say nothing at all. When people critique you personally,
face to face, take cheer; it means that they have not given
up on you yet. Only a cadaver should receive nothing
but compliments; it has no need or capacity to change or
improve. Neither a flatterer nor a flatteree be.

Charity, unlike love, is not something like a ditch into which you can fall.

43   Learn to Love Those You Don't Even Like

In modern culture, most of the ideas associated with
the concept of "love" have been subsumed under the
concepts of "preferability" and "passion." We love to eat
ice cream and we love to make love, though perhaps not
simultaneously.

The ancient Greeks primarily used three words
that have been translated "love": *philos* was brotherly
love (Monday through Friday love), *eros* was sexual love
(Saturday night love), and *agape* was a self-giving type of
love (Sunday love). The Greek authors and New Testament
writers, however, were not as consistent in their use of these
terms as philologists often claim. They occasionally used
one where we would expect the other.

Love has far more in its repertoire than merely
"liking" or being "emotionally/sexually attracted to." When
ancient Assyrian monarchs forced some weaker ruler to
enter a treaty relationship, the vassal weakling was made
to promise that he would "love" his mighty overlord. Did
the weaker ruler "like" the Assyrian tyrant? Surely not. Did
he feel an emotional attachment? Surely not. But he could
swear to "love" him, that is, to show respect and absolute
loyalty, to obey, and to aid in protecting the more powerful
king. That was love, even though the inferior probably
hated his superior's guts. Assyrian politics thus gives the
lie to the verdict of the French author, George Sand (1804–
1876) who wrote: "No human creature can give orders to
love" (*Jacques*, 1834).

In the New Testament, Jesus is quoted as saying we
should "love our enemies" (see Matthew 5:44). People
certainly do not like their enemies. They may sometimes
admire them, but admiration is not love.

The Old English term, "charity," probably reflects more
accurately what the ancients meant by love. Charity, unlike
love, is not something like a ditch into which you can fall.

"Be charitable toward your enemy" makes sense, whereas love, with its modern connotations of preferability and passion, hardly seems philologically appropriate when your enemy is the object of the verb.

We are frequently charitable, that is kindly and lenient, and even loyal, toward many people whom we don't really like, in fact, people we sometimes despise and detest: members of our own family, fellow employees and colleagues, competitors, those in authority over us, our elders, and so forth. To learn to love what we don't like means we increase that number in ever expanding circles.

To love is a decision we make, not an intuition we follow, or an infatuation that engulfs us, or a passion that enslaves us.

Our promises exceed our abilities. Our commitments exceed our performances. Our wants exceed our needs. Our expenditures exceed our resources.

44 Don't Create a Situation Where There Are More Piglets Than Teats

Animals that give birth to litters of young often create a situation of distress; there are more mouths to feed than there are faucets on the old feeding machine. A hog that gives birth to fourteen baby pigs but only possesses a dozen teats has already sentenced two to death unless there is some human intervention. The little pigs become acclimated to the same feeding spot, returning always to the nipple first claimed, and sharing is not in a piglet's vocabulary.

Our expansion beyond our capacity to perform, to feed, and to nourish has become endemic in much modern culture. Our promises exceed our abilities. Our commitments exceed our performances. Our wants exceed our needs. Our expenditures exceed our resources. An unlimited number of oinking demands hunt for nourishment from a limited number of feeder spouts. The contemporary soccer mom, who spends more time going forth and back on errands than the soccer ball moves up and down the field, has become the paradigmatic example of the overextended. But try as we may, none of us can through our own volition grow additional mammary glands nor stimulate over-challenged production from our already depleted ones.

To secure votes, politicians overextend promises that not even utopia could deliver. Manufacturers create expectations that no real product could hope to fulfill. We enlarge our indebtedness to secure our "essentials" until our personal purse strings fray. We take from one pocket to have some lining in the other. We now take from Paul to pay Peter. Overextension makes failures and ultimately liars of all its practitioners.

The answer, of course, is less. Nothing more (nor less) than less, fewer commitments, lower expectations of ourselves, our loved ones, our employees. Promising less hurts, of course. In the short run it makes us feel like less: less loving, less giving, less competent. In the long run, it means we don't have to face (or hide from) the well-deserved shame of promising what we can't deliver.

Most often, we do not give in, much less surrender, until our Watergates threaten to become our Waterloos.

45 In Our Lying Operations, Fence Construction Is Always the Costliest Expense

The ancient rabbis developed certain practices and regulations embodied in tradition that served to build "a fence around the law" (so Rabbi Akiba, about 50–135 CE, in Mishnah *Aboth* 3:14). The goal was to prevent one from coming anywhere even remotely near to transgressing a divine commandment. Eve built the first such fence in Eden when she told the snake, "We can't eat from that tree—we can't even *touch* it" (compare Genesis 2:16–17 with 3:1–3).

The laws and legislation of any culture serve as fences to protect that culture's values. Our values of social order, limited freedom, equality of opportunity, the privilege of owning property, protection of life and limb, the right to justice, and so forth are defended by numerous regulations and prohibitions. Often these may never mention the values being preserved, nor need they. Speeding laws do not exist because speeding in and of itself is bad. They are a fence around other values: the right to life and the freedom from injury.

Nowhere are more expensive fences built than in attempts to protect lapses of values, lies, mistakes, indiscretions, faux pas. Any means of coverage may appear better than daring to disclose the truth. The pattern is the same whether the offender is an ordinary person, a politician, a CEO, or a military strategist. The procedure is deny, deny, deny then lie, lie, lie. Most often, we do not give in, much less surrender, until our Watergates threaten to become our Waterloos. Many had rather die than admit a lie.

Various maneuvers may be undertaken to hide the truth or to pretend that nothing significant or consequential has been done. Most frequently, we encircle what we do not want known with hastily constructed Maginot lines, erected out of evasions, dodges, reinterpretations, equivocations, smoke screens, and prevarications. We use other, secondary lies as flying buttresses in an effort to support the sagging façade of the primary indiscretion. The flow of one lie, however, can't be dammed with a second. A lie laminated with another lie still remains transparent. The cover we lay over our failings, in the hope of hiding the truth, only highlights rather than camouflages reality. We stack misdemeanors atop our felonies in hopes that both will acquire invisibility.

One may argue for a bifurcation of life as a way of pulling the stinger from a lie: what is private is private and what is public is public; the two simply belong to different worlds and do not overlap. It does not matter if a person can't be trusted in the bedroom, one should still be listened to and believed in the parlor.

The most despicable among us are not those who knowingly do wrong but those who knowingly do wrong and experience no real sense of shame or remorse and thus no real need to even think about forgiveness.

It is amazing how easily many of us can act without any qualms of conscience. The grooves of integrity in our lives have worn so smooth that honesty has no chance of slowing down the slide of deception! Clearly many of us are members of the Already-Dead-But-Not-Yet-Buried Society.

Since we all share a common human nature and common patterns of behavior, we are usually prone to be sympathetic in our understanding and generous in our forgiveness. What is acknowledged, unless physical injury to another is involved, generally receives some level of excusability. Primary misdeeds and misstatements are considered minor in comparison with secondary fence construction, a process that moves into the category of the unforgivable. People will forgive a lie made known in the context of a request for amnesty, but they resist to the death forgiving a lie told to construct a fence around a falsehood.

Few players with unstained
uniforms ever score except
on the first play of the
game.

46 The Cleanest Uniforms Are on Those Who Play the Least

John Wesley (1703–1791), the founder of Methodism, is considered the creator of the saying, "Cleanliness is indeed next to godliness" (in *Sermon 88*, 1778, "On Dress"). He was speaking about and condemning being sloven: "slovenliness is no part of religion . . . neither this [First Peter 3:3–4] nor any text of Scripture condemns neatness of apparel; certainly this [neatness] is a duty, not a sin." For his terminology, Wesley was probably dependent upon an old listing by Rabbi Phinehas ben Jair (second century CE, quoted in Mishnah, *Sotah* 9:15, and *Midrash Rabbah* I.1:9). Though often quoted, no one can really explain how cleanliness is related to godliness other than refer to the practice of wearing clean clothing to and dressing up for attendance at worship—an idea preserved in our reference to Sunday/Sabbath dress.

Surely though, dirtiness has its place in life. If you look at the players' bench at a football game, the guys with the cleanest uniforms are those who sit out the game keeping the water boy company. Those in the rough and tumble of the play are covered with sweat, dirt, mud, grass stains, the grime of the game. Few players with unstained uniforms ever score except on the first play of the game. (This, of course, presupposes a playing field other than those constructed of artificial material or built indoors. Even on these, however, sweat happens.)

Life is a grimy business. Those whose goal is to keep their hands clean and their ascots unruffled belong on the sidelines. Adam was told that "by the sweat of your face you shall eat bread until you return to the ground (dirt), for out of it you were taken; you are dust, and to dust you shall return" (Genesis 3:19). Between the dirt from which we came and the dirt to which we shall return, we ought to live a sweaty, dirty life. We oughtn't fear engagement.

Sex is dirty, as everybody knows, so it was a dirty deed that engendered our existence. Even love itself has its dirtiness. In his play, *Look Back in Anger*, John Osborne (1929–1994) wrote: "It's no good trying to fool yourself about love. You can't fall into it like a soft job, without dirtying up your hands. It takes muscle and guts. And if you can't bear the thought of messing up your nice, clean soul, you'd better give up the whole idea of life and become a saint." There is nobility in the grime and calluses that stain and pain working hands and loving hearts. The sloppiest kiss is sometimes the best.

Politics is the art of the dirty. The highest aspirations, the noblest goals, the best intentions of a politician, all become dirtied by the ever-present need to compromise and barter. The smoke of backrooms permeates our best legislation. It is the "blood, toil, tears and sweat" (Winston Churchill, 1874–1965, addressing the House of Commons, May 13, 1940), not the clean shirt and pressed pants, that create and preserve our freedoms and guard life's benefits.

In his famous Rule, Wesley declared:

Do all the good you can,
By all the means you can,
In all the ways you can,
In all the places you can,
At all the times you can,
To all the people you can,
As long as ever you can.

You can't do all that and keep your life and clothes unstained and your bowtie straight at the same time.

Pomposity needs puncturing, inflated egos need deflating, irrationality needs ridicule.

47 The Best News Analysis Is Always on the Late Night Comedy Shows

During the Middle Ages, practically every court and prince had a court jester as a feature of their entourage. The jester was a professional clown or fool. His tasks were twofold: to entertain the court assemblies, providing diversion from the routine, and to serve as an official critic of the ruler, his staff, and policies. Jesters punctured balloons of pomposity and poked their scalpels into the crevices of illogical thought; all the time acting the clown.

With the advent of twenty-four hour news channels, the most common talking head on the telly has become the news analyst. During times of military engagement, half the retired military brass is spit-polished and ushered out of old-folk homes to appear as authorities on everything from troop deployment to weapons of mass destruction.

The need for news analysts derives from the fact that news conferences and briefings have the same air of reality about them as a World Championship Wrestling match. The ritual and the routine are there but the conformity to actuality is remote. News analysts attempt to get behind the charade. Often they, however, take themselves more seriously than the news givers and creators, arguing their positions as if the world waited for some voice from heaven, namely, theirs.

Only the late nocturnal comics are able to approach major issues and leading figures with the irreverence they deserve. These media jesters are capable of discussing the news without the accompanying anesthesia and circumlocution. Comedians are not expected to describe the clothes the king is wearing. Their task is to lift up the king's skirt and see what lies hidden underneath, and to tell us about it in such a way as not only to inform but also to entertain. Human failures, fakeries, foibles, and follies are grist for the comedian's mill. Pomposity needs puncturing, inflated egos need deflating, irrationality needs ridicule. And the burden falls on the comics. Who else?

Generally, these midnight comedians are about two months ahead of the news analysts in sensing the important and in taking the pulse of the general populace. Over against them, the news analysts appear as pompous antiquarians.

Many a face is etched with the crevices of a thousand worries.

48   Maybe Things Won't Turn Out Well: The Worrier Should at Least Receive Some Reward

Some people have often wished they could enter the minds of nonhuman creatures and think the animals' thoughts along with them. What would a creature's eye view of the world look like? Do they give thought to anything other than the immediacy of the moment? Do they worry over the unknown and suffer anxiety over the not-yet? Although not a view widely accepted, it may be that their cognitive powers differ only in degree from those of humans, but not in kind.

Does the squirrel or chipmunk, with cheeks packed to the brim, scurrying to store away nuts and seeds, ever worry whether its stash will be sufficient for the need? Do the ants and bees, those workaholics of the insect world, ever have an anxious moment over future insufficiencies? Whether they worry or not cannot be known. Perhaps it is something we should not worry about.

Humans, on the other hand, seem to possess an ample supply of worry genes. Few of us fit the *Mad Magazine* profile: "What, Me Worry?" The American physician and author Thomas Lewis (1913–1993) wrote: "We are, perhaps, unique among the earth's creatures, the worrying animal. We worry away our lives, fearing the future, discontent with the present, unable to take in the idea of dying, unable to sit still" (*The Medusa and the Snail*, 1979). Are humans the only worrying animal?

Much ink has been expended on the causes of human worrying and even more on trying to get us not to worry. An old chestnut informs us that the less we possess, the less we worry and vice versa. Rabbi Hillel (about 60 BCE—10 CE), in a less than optimistic view of life, declared: "The more flesh, the more worms. The more possessions, the more worry" (Mishnah, *Aboth* 2:7). But surely, those who have not or have less also worry.

Many glib and slick answers have been given to overcome worry. We have been extolled to "don't worry, be happy." The American clergyman and author Robert Jones Burdette (1844–1914) wrote: "There are two days in the week about which and upon which I never worry. Two carefree days, kept sacredly free from fear and apprehension. One of those days is Yesterday . . . And the other day I do not worry about is Tomorrow" (*The Golden Day*).

In the Sermon on the Mount, Jesus is said to have admonished his hearers: "Do not worry about your life, what you will eat or what you will drink, or about your body, what you will wear . . . Can any of you by worrying add a single hour to your span of life?" (Matthew 6:25, 27). Jesus, however, was not married, had no children, owned no property, had no regular job, and spent his time roaming the Palestinian countryside with a gang of unemployed misfits. Most people who repeat his advice and admonish others to observe it have made sure their job is secure and their retirement program is in order.

We probably all worry too much; especially the persons who worry in general because they have nothing in particular to worry about. Many a face is etched with the crevices of a thousand worries. The vast majority of our fears, however, never come close to becoming reality. An unattributed Irish saying declares: "It is almost impossible to exaggerate the complete unimportance of almost everything."

Anxiety over the not-yet and the not-here, however, seems as natural a part of life as a dozen other dispositions. Given life's uncertainties, crises, and disappointments, the expenditure of psychic energy devoted to worrying will probably not go unrewarded. Surely we are better off when we have worried about the right things and taken proper precautions.

Surely there is an eighth deadly sin, namely, naïveté.

49 Always Trust Your Spouse, but Hire a Good Private Investigator

We are all familiar with, and many of us practitioners of, the seven deadly sins: pride, covetousness, lust, anger, gluttony, envy, and sloth. These seven sins were first enumerated by St. Gregory the Great (540–604) in his *Moralia in Job*. Counterbalancing these vile seven are the four cardinal virtues of prudence, temperance, fortitude, and justice, first enumerated by the Greek philosophers, Plato (427–347 BCE) and Aristotle (382–322 BCE). In order to balance the score, the cardinal virtues are often supplemented by the three theological virtues of faith, hope, and love (charity).

Surely there is an eighth deadly sin, namely, naïveté. The dictionary defines "naïve" as "having or showing artless simplicity; unsophisticated; ingenuous; having or showing a lack of experience, judgment, or information." A naïve person is one who thinks the world is as one sees it, and trusts what one sees. And such a person generally sees the world as they would like it to be. Naïve vision perceives the world but without perception. It views the world through rose-colored glasses without even having to wear the glasses. It is optimistic to a fault. One naïve would buy a saddle without owning or having access to a horse. Or conquer a country assuming everybody loves a conqueror.

Perhaps no other relationship is so susceptible to naïveté as marriage. George Bernard Shaw (1856–1950) had some informative perspectives on this institution. "When two people are under the influence of the most violent, most insane, most delusive, and most transient of passions, they are required to swear that they will remain in that excited, abnormal, and exhausting condition until death do them part" (Preface to *Getting Married*, 1908). If these be the demands of marriage, then the surprise is not that half of American marriages end in divorce but that half do not.

Benjamin Franklin (1706–1790) purportedly wrote: "Keep your eyes wide open before marriage, half shut afterwards" (*Poor Richard's Almanac*, June 1738). He was extolling the necessity of choosing well before marriage, and overlooking faults and problems after the wedding. But surely his visionary recommendations should be reversed: enter marriage with your eyes half-shut and keep them wide open afterwards.

If men are hunters and women are nesters, then in marriage one may wonder, What is being hunted? And where is the nesting occurring? A good sprinkling of moderate suspicion that approaches but does not reach the level of jealousy never did a marriage harm. The spouse that is overly suspicious, however, should be suspect: "Suspicion always haunts the guilty mind; the thief doth fear each bush an officer" (William Shakespeare, 1546–1616; *King Henry the Sixth*, Part Two, 1590–1591). The suspicious is frequently the suspicionable.

Naïveté can allow the world to change under your nose and you never receive a notification nor smell how the roses have withered. The naïve often have to stumble over the world of reality. One spouse's naïveté, however, does not provide the reason but only the occasion for the other's misadventures.

Among these misadventures is spousal infidelity, the worst form of venereal disease. Like other such diseases, it is often incurable. It destroys the health of the one flesh that matrimony creates. Even to think of one's spouse or lover embraced in another's arms can create the pain of an unanesthesized visceral excavation. In our imagination, the sounds and moans we hear are not just those of illicit lovers; they are the reverberations of a heart strangulating from sorrow. A country songster might croon: "You are forever *on* my mind but so often *in* the arms of someone else." No sword pierces and slices the heart like that drawn and wielded by the one you love. It can shatter the sleep of the naïve.

The Roman satirical poet Juvenal (55–130 CE) wrote: "The husband is the last to know the dishonor of his house" (*Satires*). Perhaps men are more naïve than women.

To misquote the English classicist and poet, A. E. Housman (1859–1936): "Give crowns and pounds and guineas and even your heart away" but hold back at least a pocketful of suspicion. Keep both your heart and eyes open toward your significant other lest you yourself become an insignificant other. Have confidence and trust in your other. But scrutinize the evidence with care.

The present generation lives and guards itself and its privileges by mortgaging or expending the next.

50 If You are Young, Worry about the Laius not the Oedipus Complex

In Greek legend, told by Sophocles (c. 495–406 BCE), the king of Thebes, Laius, and his wife, Jocasta, gave birth to a son. Because of a prediction that he would slay his father, the child was exposed with his feet tied and a nail piercing them. Found by a shepherd, the child was raised at another court and given the name Oedipus meaning "swollen feet." Eventually Oedipus unknowingly killed his father and married his mother by whom he fathered children. When the truth was learned, his mother/wife hanged herself and Oedipus went into exile.

The legend of Oedipus provided the structural framework for a psychoanalytic theory called the Oedipus Complex. According to this theory, a male child, while still very young, has sexual desires for the mother, which of course leads to fear of the father who is viewed as dangerous, hostile, and a rival to be eliminated. The boy resolves this dilemma by identifying with the feared father, abandoning his romantic attachment to his mother, and redirecting his erotic interests outside the family. (The counterpart, in which the daughter desires the father and wishes to replace the mother, is called the Electra Complex. It differs in important respects from the male version.) These positive sexual feelings toward the parent of the opposite sex and the ambivalent hostile feelings toward those of the same sex are normally relinquished or repressed but they have the potential for producing neurotic conflict. A simplified, popular form of this theory simply sees the younger generation as out to replace and take over from the older generation.

Just as Oedipus had a father problem, so Laius had a son problem. Laius set out to protect himself by disposing of his son. Like Laius, every generation can choose to defend and enhance itself at the expense of the next. This could be called the Laius Complex. According to this theory, the present generation lives and guards itself and its privileges by mortgaging or expending the next. The operation of this complex can be seen not only in warfare but also in general generational indulgence.

Long ago, people recognized that wars were fought and won by the older generation on the backs of and at the price of the lives of the younger generation. King Croesus of Lydia, about 560 BCE, supposedly wrote to a king of Persia: "Peace is better than war, because in peace the sons bury their fathers, but in war the fathers bury their sons." In his history, the Greek historian Herodotus (about 485–425 BCE) said about the same thing: "In peace, children inter their parents; war violates the order of nature and causes parents to inter their children." Herbert Hoover (1874–1964), addressing the Republican National Convention (June 27, 1944), made even more obvious this factor: "Older men declare war. But it is youth that must fight and die. And it is youth who must inherit the tribulation, the sorrow, and the triumphs that are the aftermath of war."

In the ancient world, child sacrifice and, especially, the exposure of infants were used to reduce the demands of the future upon the present. Among the hundreds of ancient Greek papyri discovered in the dry sands of Egypt is one containing a letter from a laborer to his wife. The man had left home and gone to Alexandria to find work. His letter notes that he had been successful and would soon send funds to his wife. At the end of the letter is a pathetic note that tells the woman, already long pregnant, that when the child arrives, if it is a son to keep it but if it is a daughter to expose it. A son held promise of providing for the father, a daughter would be a burden; her future would only diminish the family's present, being another mouth to feed, another body to clothe, and another female to try and marry off.

Today we no longer sanction child sacrifice nor death through exposure. In securing our goals and defending our present, however, we still endanger the lives of the young: land mines, cluster bombs, and uranium-laden shells are not only means used for our protection but also endangerments for our children.

People watch, teary-eyed, as the young graduate, the recently married, and the new father or mother go off to war, some eventually to fall on foreign soil and to leave forever unfillable tombs in the hearts of those who waved them goodbye. The older generation, in a cause they did not understand and to a war they knew could not be won, sent its youth in full bloom to the conflict in Viet Nam, that Asian quagmire eight thousand miles from home and half a step from Hell. Wars are old men's games they force their children to play.

The Laius Complex not only finds embodiment in war but also in other matters as well. The present generation can splurge itself economically and environmentally at the expense of generations yet to come. By preserving ourselves, our living standards, our comfort zones, and our values, and by overusing resources to meet our needs and wants, we may endanger those yet to be. The older generation charges its indulgences and places its irresponsibilities on the credit cards of its children. We make hogs of ourselves on funds looted from our children's piggy banks.

Cursed be the generation that would feather its nest with down plucked from the breasts of its offspring.

*If the Creator . . . produced
it and perpetuates it,
making all things new every
morning, let us feel an
obligation to acknowledge
it; don't ignore it as a vista
unseen.*

51 Appreciate the Fact that the Whole of Creation Was Made Just for You

In the Jewish Mishnah (from about 200 CE), there is a passage that reads as follows: "Man stamps many coins with the one seal and they are all like one another; but the King of kings, the Holy One, blessed is he, has stamped every man with the seal of the first man, yet not one of them is like his fellow. Therefore every one must say, 'For my sake was the world created'" (*Sanhedrin* 4:5). This statement affirms that all humans are like the first human but every human being is different from every other human being. Because each is of the same species but each a unique specimen, each of us can claim that the world was made just for my sake.

Such a self-centered view of the universe may appear to be overly egotistical, narcissistic, self-centered, and conceited. Most of these qualities have been roundly condemned throughout the years. The American clergyman Henry Ward Beecher (1813–1887), for example, wrote "conceit is the most incurable disease that is known to the human soul" (*Proverbs from Plymouth Pulpit,* 1887).

Perhaps, however, we should not read this old mishnaic statement as one of mere conceit nor of rampant self-centeredness. Why not read it as a statement of ego-strength building and even an expression of self-assurance? The world was made for your enjoyment, for your appreciation, for your work, and for your rest.

The blazing sunset with fiery red fingers massaging the sky: . . . just for you! The momentary flare of a shooting star fire-etching the night: . . . just for you! The newly born comforted against its mother's breast exuding the promise of continued life: . . . just for you! The streaking heat of a lightning bolt and its reverberating clap of thunder: . . . just for you! The vista of snow-capped mountains with riverlets furrowing their sides: . . . just for you! The thick black sky, sequined with diamond-like stars, stretching on everywhere and forever: . . . just for you! The enticing odor of newly baked yeasted bread: . . . just for you! The bouquet of an old wine aged to perfection: . . . just for you! The invigorating taste of morning's first cup of coffee: . . . just for you! The Shakespearean sonnet that thrills the soul: . . . just for you! The play of wind dancing through the treetops: . . . just for you! The blossoming of flowers on a cool, spring day: . . . just for you! The crisp fall day when the leaves on the trees are splattered with extravagance: . . . just for you! The new snowfall that overnight transforms the world into a trackless wilderness: . . . just for you!

On an early winter morning, shortly after the crack of dawn and with a chill in the air and frost kissing the earth, I found myself lying flat on the ground. In front of me, fully prone, lay a would-be mother, a young heifer carrying her firstborn. Tresses, so-called because of her curly hair hanging where horns could have grown, had struggled for hours to deliver. Before I arrived, she had given up on giving birth and lay there unmoving, waiting to die.

The young calf had chewed its tongue while trying to exit its mother. Its mouth was full of coagulated blood. I attached pull cords to its protruding feet. Pushing against the cow's body with my feet, I pulled and struggled to free it. Nothing gave for at least five minutes. Gaining a second wind, I exerted to the fullest and felt the first slip of the calf whom I assumed was long dead. Within fifteen seconds, the well-lubricated calf had emerged, dragged from its mother's body. To my surprise, the calf opened its big eyes. I quickly cleared its mouth, rammed fingers down its throat, and listened to it take its first gargling breath. Sitting in the cold that morning, exhausted, I knew one thing: those batting eyes and gargling breath . . . just for me.

If the world with all its wonders was made just for you and me, let us receive it as a gift, embrace it as a prize, cherish it as a treasure, enjoy it as a partner, respect it as a relative, explore it as a mystery, and nurture it as an offspring. If the Creator (or even time and chance, circumstance and mutation) produced it and perpetuates it, making all things new every morning, let us feel an obligation to acknowledge it; don't ignore it as a vista unseen. Fall in love with the world. Give it a long look, for in what you see you may see yourself.

As Alice Walker (1944–) wrote of her favorite pigment: "I think it pisses God off if you walk by the color purple in a field somewhere and don't notice it" (*The Color Purple*, 1982). We should all be pissed off at ourselves if we let the world go past and we don't sit up and take notice. It is just for you, and just for me!

Let's live with honesty
and integrity so we won't
stagger through the twilight
of our days with a heart
clogged with remorse.

52 History Never Repeats Itself; We have to Try to Live It Right the Only Time Around

Two Greek thinkers, so the story goes, were standing beside a slowly flowing stream discussing the nature of reality. Expounding a philosophy of eternal return, one said to the other: "Some day, in that infinite future, we shall stand again as we stand today and dip our toes in the same water that now flows." Oh to God that such was the case, and we could stand there knowing that already we had dipped our digits into this water deep and had watched the rippling consequences such an action produced.

Nothing could be farther from the truth. Instead, time like a river bears all its children away and we can only glance over our shoulder as the past recedes and watch as the shadows engulf and obscure what was but which will never be again. All too soon, all our tomorrows become our yesterdays. So soon, our long view of life is in the rearview mirror.

In modern times, the Spanish-born American philosopher George Santayana (1863–1952) gave expression to and popularized the idea that history repeats itself: "Those who cannot remember the past are condemned to repeat it" (*The Life of Reason*, 1905–1906). Repetition of the past is, of course, an impossibility; that we perform actions similar and analogous to those in the past, however, is true. Both Napoleon and Hitler sent their military might into Russia and both their armies became entrapped in winter's killing blast. But Napoleon was Napoleon and Hitler was Hitler. In history, there may be rhymes, rhythms, and analogies, but not repetitions. The present may mirror the past, but the mirror provides an image, not the real thing.

That history happens in unrepeatable linearity means we must take its course and our participation in its movement with utmost seriousness and ultimate finality.

There is no instant nor delayed replay. Santayana's adage does not negate Omar Khayyám's insight:

> The Moving Finger writes; and, having writ,
> Moves on: nor all your Piety nor Wit
> Shall lure it back to cancel half a Line,
> Nor all your Tears wash out a Word of it.
> (*The Rubáiyat of Omar Khayyám*, stanza 71)

If the universe has been around for billions of years and humans for thousands of years, then our brief existence of, hopefully, threescore and ten, or if strong, perhaps fourscore years (see Psalm 90:10), is only one small scene in the cosmic slide show of existence, one little flicker in the Milky Way's galaxy, one little hiccup in a class-five hurricane, one infinitesimal grain in the sands of an infinite cosmic beach, one tiny nodular floater in an ever-flowing, never-slowing stream of DNA.

We are all bit players in a narrative, the plot of which we shall never know. But it's all we've got, and we can't afford not to take it seriously and not do the best we can. Because it's all we've got we must treasure and respect it all the more. We must hold it close, embrace it like a child hugging a stuffed animal, but avoid suffocating it. We must suck out every lingering ounce of life's sweet savor like a fluttering hummingbird loots the last ooze of nectar from summer's final flower.

At the inauguration of Bill Clinton, January 20, 1993, Maya Angelou (1928–) read her poem, *On the Pulse of Morning*. In it she wrote:

> History, despite its wrenching pain,
> Cannot be unlived, but if faced
> With courage, need not be lived again.

Courage helps us perform the unrepeatable.

To misquote the American poet, John Greenleaf Whittier (1807–1892): "For of all sad words of tongue or pen, the saddest are these: You can't do it again" (*Maud Muller*, 1864). Or to parallel that baseball philosopher, Yogi

Berra (1925–): "When it's over, it's over." Let's try and make the most of our existence. Let's give it our best, appreciate its every moment, and enjoy it to the fullest. Let's live with honesty and integrity so we won't stagger through the twilight of our days with a heart clogged with remorse. We should live life by what is right, not by what we can keep out of sight.

When we leave life behind, may we be able to do so with no regret and no apology. May we leave our space uncluttered for the next occupant, with little or no trace of our personal trash.

And when on our day the sun has set, let us pray that the darkness be not long delayed, that short will be that evening journey into night. And may that night kiss us softly on the cheek, and embrace us tenderly in its keep.

Index of Authors

About the Author

The seventh of eight children born into an Alabama sharecropper's home, the author was ordained as a Southern Baptist minister on November 9, 1952. He received a BA degree from Howard College (now Samford University) in 1956 and has served as a minister in Baptist churches in Alabama, Kentucky, and New Jersey. As a Fulbright scholar, he attended New College, Edinburgh in 1956–1957. After studying at The Southern Baptist Seminary in Louisville (1957–1958), he received a BD degree (1960) and a PhD from Princeton Theological Seminary (1964). He is the father of two daughters and one son.

The author, co-author, and editor of over forty books, he taught at Trinity University in San Antonio (1964–1972) and recently retired from the Candler School of Theology at Emory University, where he was the Franklin N. Parker Professor of Old Testament and Professor of Hebrew Bible in Emory's Graduate Division of Religion.

Since 1992, he has lived on and operated a small beef-cattle farm in Chambers County, Alabama.